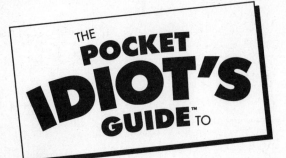

THE
POCKET
IDIOT'S
GUIDE™ TO

Home Buying Checklists

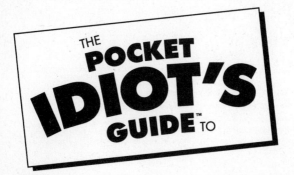

THE POCKET IDIOT'S GUIDE TO

Home Buying Checklists

by Marcia Layton Turner

ALPHA

A member of Penguin Group (USA) Inc.

ALPHA BOOKS

Published by the Penguin Group

Penguin Group (USA) Inc., 375 Hudson Street, New York, New York 10014, USA

Penguin Group (Canada), 90 Eglinton Avenue East, Suite 700, Toronto, Ontario M4P 2Y3, Canada (a division of Pearson Penguin Canada Inc.)

Penguin Books Ltd., 80 Strand, London WC2R 0RL, England

Penguin Ireland, 25 St. Stephen's Green, Dublin 2, Ireland (a division of Penguin Books Ltd.)

Penguin Group (Australia), 250 Camberwell Road, Camberwell, Victoria 3124, Australia (a division of Pearson Australia Group Pty. Ltd.)

Penguin Books India Pvt. Ltd., 11 Community Centre, Panchsheel Park, New Delhi—110 017, India

Penguin Group (NZ), 67 Apollo Drive, Rosedale, North Shore, Auckland 1311, New Zealand (a division of Pearson New Zealand Ltd.)

Penguin Books (South Africa) (Pty.) Ltd., 24 Sturdee Avenue, Rosebank, Johannesburg 2196, South Africa

Penguin Books Ltd., Registered Offices: 80 Strand, London WC2R 0RL, England

Copyright © 2009 by Marcia Layton Turner

THE POCKET IDIOT'S GUIDE TO and Design are trademarks of Penguin Group (USA) Inc.

International Standard Book Number: 978-1-59257-810-8
Library of Congress Catalog Card Number: 2008931265

11   10   09   8   7   6   5   4   3   2   1

Interpretation of the printing code: The rightmost number of the first series of numbers is the year of the book's printing; the rightmost number of the second series of numbers is the number of the book's printing. For example, a printing code of 09-1 shows that the first printing occurred in 2009.

Printed in the United States of America

Note: This publication contains the opinions and ideas of its author. It is intended to provide helpful and informative material on the subject matter covered. It is sold with the understanding that the author and publisher are not engaged in rendering professional services in the book. If the reader requires personal assistance or advice, a competent professional should be consulted.

The author and publisher specifically disclaim any responsibility for any liability, loss, or risk, personal or otherwise, which is incurred as a consequence, directly or indirectly, of the use and application of any of the contents of this book.

Contents

4 Your Dream Home 49

5 Contenders 65

7 Digging for Answers   99

Introduction

Congratulations on your decision to buy a new home! In addition to improving your financial net worth, owning your home means you can decorate it to your taste and paint it whatever colors you like. Often, you can also tackle bigger projects like adding a backyard patio, taking out a wall between rooms, or putting down new kitchen flooring.

But before you start redecorating, you'll need to find that perfect home. This book can help. Designed to make the home buying process simpler and easier, *The Pocket Idiot's Guide to Home Buying Checklists* is a useful tool to carry with you to every home you tour.

Working chapter by chapter, you can navigate the sometimes confusing process of buying real estate. First you'll determine how much you can spend on a home, and then you'll start looking, narrowing your search until you settle on the home that will best meet your needs, now and for the foreseeable future. After you zero in on a home you want to buy, you can use the checklists and forms here to organize the paperwork and create a closing and move-in schedule.

Have fun!

How This Book Is Organized

This book is presented in nine chapters:

Chapter 1, "What Can You Afford?" helps you determine what you can realistically afford to pay for your first home. By leading you through the process of tallying your income sources, totaling your monthly expenses, and compiling your available down payment funds, you can get a rough estimate of how much home you can comfortably buy. The chapter also covers preparing for the preapproval process, which you'll want to do before you start home shopping. Finally, you'll get some tips on checking out possible real estate agents to find the best match.

Chapter 2, "Starting Your Geographic Search," leads you through the process of evaluating the cities and towns nearby to locate the general area you want to live in. Now that you know approximately how much you have to spend, you can rule out some areas and rule others in. You'll also want to take a look at the rate of appreciation, property taxes, crime, school quality, and other factors.

Chapter 3, "Scoping Out Neighborhoods," is the chapter where you start to narrow down your search to the neighborhood level. From studying the advantages and disadvantages of certain neighborhoods, to evaluating size and safety, to checking out school quality, this chapter leads you step by step through the evaluation.

Chapter 4, "Your Dream Home," helps you figure out exactly what you want and need in your first home. Which features are the must-haves and which are the nice-to-haves? Are you willing to tackle a fixer-upper or is a move-in-ready newer home more your style? Through a series of questions here, you'll begin to picture the perfect home for you.

Chapter 5, "Contenders," is designed to aid you in keeping track of which home features and amenities you like most in the homes you've toured. After you've been through a few, it becomes harder and harder to remember whether the home on Main Street had a fireplace or not, or whether it was maybe the home on Maple Avenue. Take note of your favorite homes here.

In **Chapter 6, "Local Comparables,"** you'll start to compare your top picks with homes that have recently sold, to get a sense of what a fair price would be for the homes you've seen. You may discover that the asking price of one home is below market value while another is significantly overpriced. Looking at comparables, or comps, provided by your real estate agent can be quite eye-opening.

Chapter 7, "Digging for Answers," arms you with tips for researching homes you like, to see what you can find out about the homes' recent owners, their motivation for selling, and how willing to negotiate they may be. It's all about doing your research.

Chapter 8, "The Finalists," covers the final steps in deciding which home to buy. When you locate one or more homes you may be interested in buying that are within your price range, it's time to start considering the cost to own each one. Will you need to do some updating? Are there condition issues you'll need to address before moving in? These are all factors you'll want to weigh *before* making an official offer to purchase.

Chapter 9, "Countdown to Closing," leads you through the remaining steps in making an offer, scheduling a home inspection, and planning for your closing and move. Using the checklists here, you'll be well prepared to take the plunge, and you'll have help in avoiding common pitfalls.

Appendixes A and B contain a glossary of commonly used real estate terms and a list of additional helpful resources.

Things to Help You Out Along the Way

Throughout the chapters, you will notice some special messages along the way:

> Helpful hints and useful resources will be mentioned within these little boxes. From ideas to save you money to websites that put information at your fingertips, you won't want to overlook these important nuggets.

Acknowledgments

A big thank you goes to my wonderful and talented editor, Michele Wells, who helped make this manuscript even stronger. The editorial team at Alpha, including Phil Kitchel, Janette Lynn, and Andy Saff, made sure the material was both comprehensive and interesting, as well as free of obvious grammatical and typographical errors.

Rochester real estate agent extraordinaire Terri Ross provided plenty of material and guidance along the way, proving once again why she's a sales superstar.

Finally, a thank you goes to my family, who supported my work and long hours. Charlie, Grant, and Amanda, you're the best!

Special Thanks to the Technical Reviewer

The Pocket Idiot's Guide to Home Buying Checklists was reviewed by an expert who double-checked the accuracy of what you'll learn here, to help us ensure that this book gives you everything you need to know about home buying. Special thanks are extended to Bridget McCrea.

Bridget was a joy to work with. She brought her experience as a former real estate agent and frequent author to bear on this project and I am forever indebted.

Trademarks

What Can You Afford?

In This Chapter

- Calculating your home buying budget
- Smart financial moves to make before you buy
- Familiarizing yourself with the process
- Choosing a real estate agent

There are hundreds—perhaps even thousands—of properties on the market today in your area. It's likely your next home is among them, but until you spend a little time crunching some numbers, you won't know what price range you should be looking at.

Tallying your income and subtracting your monthly obligations will give you a general idea of what size mortgage you may qualify for. You won't know for certain until you actually fill out the paperwork at a bank or mortgage broker's office, but the general checklists in this chapter should get you in the ballpark. However, the size mortgage you qualify for and the size you are comfortable with may be two very different numbers, so you'll want to think about both before you start touring homes.

Income Sources

Unless you intend to pay cash for your next home, you'll need to apply for a mortgage to finance its cost. One thing your banker or mortgage broker will want to see is how much money you have coming in on a regular basis. Here is a checklist to help you add it all up:

How much do you make each month?		
Income	You	Co-borrower
Alimony	_____	_____
Bonuses	_____	_____
Child support	_____	_____
Commissions	_____	_____
Dividend/interest income	_____	_____
Investment income	_____	_____
Loans made and being repaid	_____	_____
Overtime	_____	_____
Pension	_____	_____
Required IRA withdrawal	_____	_____
Rental property income	_____	_____
Second job salary/pay	_____	_____
Social services/Social Security	_____	_____
Take-home salary (net amount)	_____	_____
Other income	_____	_____
Total Income	_____	_____
Total Income Combined (add both borrowers)	_____	

One caveat, however, is that any income you want considered in your application must be assured for at least three more years. So if you're currently receiving child support, for example, but it ends in less than three years, it won't count as income for the mortgage. The same goes for investment or other income as well.

> Before you apply for a mortgage, take a minute to check your credit report for mistakes. Thanks to the Fair and Accurate Credit Transactions (FACT) Act, the three major credit reporting agencies Equifax (www.equifax.com), Experian (www. experian.com), and TransUnion (www.transunion. com) are required to give you one free credit report each year.

Expenses

Nearly as important as what you earn is how much you of it you spend each month. In particular, lenders look at your non-housing expenses, and so should you as you start to prepare a budget. One-time purchases need not be included, but ongoing obligations should be.

What do you spend?		
Expenses	You	Co-borrower
Alimony		
Car insurance		
Car payment		

continues

What do you spend? (continued)		
Expenses	You	Co-borrower
Child care		
Child support		
Clothing		
Club/organizational dues		
Credit card payments		
Education/tuition		
Entertainment		
Food and supplies		
Loans		
Medical insurance		
Personal care		
Student loans		
Telephone, cable, Internet		
Tithing/church pledge		
Travel/vacations		
Other expenses		
Total Expenses		
Total Expenses Combined (add both borrowers)		

Twenty-five percent of your gross income used was once the recommended maximum for housing costs. So, for example, if you made $4,000 a month, you would shoot to spend no more than $1,000 on housing. Today that rule isn't carved in stone, especially with the appreciation some markets have witnessed, but it's still a decent guideline to use.

Housing Budget

Historically, mortgage companies used a loan-to-income ratio to determine how large a mortgage you could afford. Loan-to-income simply refers to the percentage of your total monthly income that you are allowed to commit to your mortgage—somewhere between 28 and 36 percent.

Today, however, your credit rating plays a much larger role in determining how large a mortgage you'll qualify for. That means you need to determine what percent of your income you're comfortable devoting to housing costs.

To determine how much income you have each month to dedicate to a mortgage, all you need to do is a little subtraction:

How much do you have available for housing?

Total income combined (from the first table)	_____
- Subtract total expenses combined (from the second table)	_____
= Remaining monthly income available for housing	_____

According to the Bureau of Labor Statistics' report "100 Years of Consumer Spending," in 2002, the average American family spent 50.1 percent of its total income on food, clothing, and housing.

Actual Costs of Homeownership

Although as a renter your housing cost probably consisted of the rent payment and utilities, as a homeowner, there are many additional costs. On top of your mortgage payment, you also need to set aside money for:

- Property taxes
- Homeowners insurance
- Condo or homeowners' association fees
- Utilities
- Maintenance and repairs
- Appliance replacement

As you start to evaluate different properties, you'll want to be sure to factor these additional costs into your decision.

Down-Payment Sources

Another factor is how much money you have to use as a down payment on your first home. Use the following fill-in-the-blank section to add up your assets.

In many cases, you can tap into your retirement funds without penalty if you're buying a home. However, some may require you to repay whatever you've borrowed within a certain amount of time or risk getting hit with a withdrawal penalty.

How much can you put down?

Savings	_____
Stocks and bonds	_____
401k/retirement fund borrowing	_____
Gifts	_____
Commissions/bonuses due	_____
Other funds	_____
Total Down-Payment Funds	_____

Obviously, the more you can put down up front to pay for your first home, the more house you can buy—or, the lower your mortgage payment on the home you fell in love with.

Mortgage Payments

Once you know how much money you can spend on housing—your mortgage payment plus other home-related expenses—you can begin estimating the size mortgage you want. Amortization tables can help with that, by telling you how much you'll pay each month for every $1,000 you borrow.

The key facts you need to have available are the following:

How much will your mortgage cost?

Amount of mortgage	_____
Current interest rate	_____
Term of mortgage (5, 10, 15, 20, 30, 40 years)	_____

If you're not sure what the average interest rate is for mortgages in your area, you can check out a number of websites that will tell you. Some popular ones include:

> **Freddie Mac's Market Report:**
> www.freddiemac.com/dlink/html/PMMS/
> display/PMMSOutputYr.jsp
>
> **Mortgage 101 Daily Rate Averages:**
> www.mortgage101.com/Articles/
> DailyRateSurvey.asp
>
> **Yahoo! Real Estate:**realestate.yahoo.com/loans

Keep in mind that your credit score drastically affects what mortgage lenders will charge you. The higher your interest rate, the higher your monthly mortgage payment. So while the national average may be 6 percent, if your credit score is low you may get stuck with a rate closer to 6.5 or 7 percent.

To calculate approximately how much a certain size mortgage will cost every month at the going interest rate, turn to an online calculator such as the ones at www.bankrate.com/brm/ mortgage-calculator.asp or www.bloomberg. com/invest/calculators/mortgage.html.

Prepping for the Purchase

Even before you start searching in earnest for your dream home, there are steps you should take to shore up your financial situation. By curbing expenses, paying down debt, and fixing any credit report errors, you'll position yourself to get the least expensive mortgage you can. Use this checklist to make sure you've done all the necessary prep work:

How can you clean up your financial house before applying for a mortgage?

☐ Check your credit, or FICO, score.

☐ Correct any credit report errors you discover.

☐ If you've had one or two late payments with a credit card company, ask for a "goodwill adjustment" to get them erased.

☐ Make sure your true available credit amount is correct on the report if it is higher than what the report shows.

☐ Pay off credit cards, especially those with small balances remaining.

☐ Don't open any new accounts.

☐ Don't close any accounts, or you will reduce the total amount of credit you have available, which lowers your FICO score.

Home buyers who put less than 20 percent down at closing are charged private mortgage insurance (PMI), which can add up to hundreds or thousands of dollars a year, depending on the size of your mortgage. To avoid this charge and save yourself some money, do all you can to put at least 20 percent down on your home.

If you'll be moving from a home or apartment that you rent, you'll also want to do the following:

How should you get ready for a move?

☐ Read through your rental agreement to understand how much notification you must give your landlord before moving out.

☐ Time your home search to coincide with a lease ending date, two to four months in advance.

☐ Begin taking care of any minor repairs you are responsible for making to the unit.

☐ As soon as you have a closing date for your new home, notify your landlord of your intent not to renew.

☐ If you need more time because your closing has been delayed, ask to continue renting month to month.

☐ Request your security deposit back once your apartment has been inspected and approved.

There is a big difference between being prequalified and preapproved for a mortgage. Being prequalified is simply having an estimate of how large a mortgage you'll be approved for, whereas being preapproved means that a lender has committed to lending you up to a maximum amount. You want to go the extra mile and be preapproved.

Preapproval Process

One of the first questions real estate agents will likely ask you is, "How much have you been preapproved for?" Your response will confirm that you, in fact, have been preapproved, and that you're serious about a purchase. It also gives them a price range to start researching for you.

But before you rush to get preapproved by your current bank, do some research on the going rate to ensure you get the best deal. Since rates fluctuate daily, do your comparison right before you intend to apply for preapproval:

How should you compare mortgage lenders?			
Details	Lender #1	#2	#3
Rate	_____	_____	_____
Term (10, 15, 30 years)	_____	_____	_____
Fixed or adjustable rate mortgage (ARM)	_____	_____	_____
Points	_____	_____	_____
Early payoff penalty	_____	_____	_____
Application fee	_____	_____	_____
Lock-in period	_____	_____	_____
Closing costs	_____	_____	_____
Conversion option (to fixed rate)	_____	_____	_____

Getting preapproved isn't all that involved, but it does require pulling together some paperwork to present to the mortgage lender you intend to use:

Paperwork to give to the mortgage lender
☐ Last year's tax return
☐ A recent pay stub
☐ Copies of checking account statements
☐ Copies of investment account statements
☐ Permission to run a credit check on you

Surprisingly, your credit score will improve if you have a little bit of money charged on several credit cards rather than a lot of money charged on only a few. Spread out your spending to avoid the appearance that you've maxed out a card.

Evaluating Possible Agents

Real estate agents and brokers are excellent sources of information about available homes. Finding a good one can help you quickly identify neighborhoods and streets of interest, as well as homes that meet all of your needs. So what are some questions you should ask potential agents before agreeing to work with them?

How should you select the best real estate agent for you?

Issues	Agent #1	#2	#3
How many years have you been selling real estate?	___	___	___
Have you earned any awards or special designations for your performance?	___	___	___
Are you primarily a listing or selling agent?	___	___	___
Do you work alone or as part of a team?	___	___	___
How many homes did you sell last year?	___	___	___
How many homes did you sell last month?	___	___	___
Were they primarily single family houses, townhouses, condos, or commercial property?	___	___	___
What is the average price of homes you've sold in the last three months?	___	___	___
What is the price range of those homes you sold?	___	___	___
What areas or neighborhoods do you primarily work in?	___	___	___
What percent of your clients are first-time home buyers?	___	___	___
Will you also work as a buyer's broker?	___	___	___
Do you charge any up-front fees for your services?	___	___	___

continues

How should you select the best real estate agent for you? (continued)			
Issues	Agent #1	#2	#3
How often do you communicate with your clients while they're actively looking for a home?	___	___	___
What one thing sets you apart from other top agents?	___	___	___
Other than you, who is the best real estate agent in town and why?	___	___	___
What else should I know about you that you haven't yet told me?	___	___	___

> Although no one likes to be in debt, mortgage debt actually has tax benefits. The interest you pay on your mortgage is fully tax deductible, unlike other types of debt.

These questions will help you assess how equipped each agent is to assist you in your home search.

There is no real right or wrong answer, but what you hear in response to your questions can help you choose an agent who best matches your needs, familiarity with the process, and personality. And personality is important, because you need to feel very comfortable sharing your lifestyle and habits with the agent in order to find the best home. If you don't click, don't select that agent!

It may help to rank your expectations and priorities with respect to your real estate agent in order to find one who best matches up. Assign a value of 1 to 10, with 1 being the most important, to each of these descriptions and work habits:

Who is your perfect real estate agent?

Rank 1-10

_____ Responsive—returns calls in a matter of minutes

_____ Accessible—nearly always available by phone or e-mail

_____ Knowledgeable—well informed about the home-buying process and our top neighborhood choices

_____ Aggressive—willing to bend over backward to get you the home you want

_____ Plugged in—well connected in the real estate world with other professionals you'll need

_____ Experienced—has closed hundreds or thousands of sales

_____ Friendly—easy to talk to, reassuring, and supportive

_____ Communicative—willing to share information about homes, neighborhoods, and pros and cons

_____ Honest—won't break the rules or act unethically but shares his or her opinions

_____ Creative—has excellent problem-solving skills and is likely to find a way to get you what you want

Sometimes prioritizing what you're looking for in an agent can help you pick the one who has the skills and traits you know you want.

Questions to Ask Your Mortgage Broker/Real Estate Agent

What should I be doing now to prepare for buying a home?

_____

_____

Are there any special mortgage programs for first-time buyers I might qualify for that would give me a better interest rate?

_____

_____

Do you see any potential problems with my getting approved for a mortgage?

_____

_____

If yes, is there anything I can do to address those issues now?

_____

_____

Which mortgage lenders do you typically recommend for first-time buyers?

_____

_____

Notes/Observations

_____

_____

_____

_____

_____

_____

_____

_____

_____

_____

_____

_____

_____

_____

_____

_____

_____

_____

_____

_____

_____

Starting Your Geographic Search

In This Chapter

- Defining your perfect locale
- Sorting through amenities
- Tracking down crime stats
- Assessing school performance

Now you know how much you can afford to spend on your first home and it's time to start checking out properties. There are plenty to choose from, but to avoid looking at every one, you'll want to think about the kind of area you want to live in.

Rural or urban? Mature or up and coming? Large town or small village? These are the kinds of questions it will help to answer up front. You and/or your real estate agent will have a much easier time finding your first place if you can describe the type of locale you want to call home.

Cities, Towns, and Villages

In any city or town, a reputation develops. Maybe it's the area where the wealthy are known to buy, or has the best schools, the nicest downtown, or the lowest taxes. Every area has its perceived pros or cons, and now it's your turn to weigh them for yourself. What kind of immediate area are you looking to call home? What are your priorities?

What kind of area do you want to call home?
☐ Downtown
☐ Suburb
☐ Town
☐ Village
☐ Hamlet
☐ Countryside
☐ The best schools
☐ Good schools
☐ Low crime
☐ Diverse population
☐ Large population (more than 500,000 residents)
☐ Small population (fewer than 20,000 residents)
☐ Primarily Republican
☐ Primarily Democratic
☐ Lower-cost homes
☐ Moderately priced homes
☐ Upscale homes
☐ Historic homes
☐ Newer homes

At Sperling's Best Places, at www.bestplaces.net, you can check out the cost of living, schools, and crime, and gather more information about the pros and cons of a particular city.

Property Tax Rates

Each state sets its own property tax rate by county and town, so you'll want to check with your local assessor's office to determine the exact tax rate for your area. However, here are some rough guidelines for what you can expect for your state and how it compares with others:

What is your state's property tax rate?

Alabama: .65	Idaho: 1.42
Alaska: 1.80	Illinois: 1.79
Arizona: 1.21	Indiana: 2.12
Arkansas: .88	Iowa: 2.15
California: .68	Kansas: 2.09
Colorado: 1.08	Kentucky: .96
Connecticut: 1.72	Louisiana: 1.02
Delaware: .68	Maine: 1.75
District of	Maryland: 1.06
Columbia: 1.31	Massachusetts: 1.07
Florida: 1.20	Michigan: 1.91
Georgia: 1.52	Minnesota: 1.27
Hawaii: .40	Mississippi: 1.44

Missouri: 1.42

Montana: 1.65

Nebraska: 2.15

Nevada: .83

New Hampshire: 2.21

New Jersey: 1.78

New Mexico: .72

New York: 1.76

North Carolina: 1.10

North Dakota: 1.84

Ohio: 1.81

Oklahoma: 1.03

Oregon: 1.22

Pennsylvania: 1.70

Rhode Island: 1.52

South Carolina: 1.38

South Dakota: 1.96

Tennessee: 1.07

Texas: 2.57

Utah: 1.31

Vermont: 2.06

Virginia: 1.12

Washington: 1.13

West Virginia: .95

Wisconsin: 2.09

Wyoming: 2.18

U.S. average: 1.38

Source: Moody's Economy.com

Taking advantage of any property tax relief programs your state offers will help reduce your annual property tax bill. Ask your real estate agent about such programs and how you can apply. (New York State's STAR program is one of the most well-known.)

Percent Increase in Taxes

Property tax rates change based on two factors: funds needed to support the municipality's or city's financial needs and a change in a property's assessed value.

What kinds of increases have towns around you witnessed both in the base tax rate and local assessments? Use the form to take notes.

What tax rate changes have occurred in your town?			
Area	Current Tax Rate	Tax Rate Change (1 yr)	Tax Rate Change (5 yr)
_____	_____	_____	_____
_____	_____	_____	_____
_____	_____	_____	_____

Resale Values

To know how well homes in a particular locale are selling, you'll need the help of your real estate agent, who has access to property sale information going back several years.

Use this fill-in-the-blanks page to note how well property in your top five choices of towns are appreciating.

How is property appreciating in your preferred areas?	
Area	Appreciation Rate (1 yr)
_____	_____
_____	_____
_____	_____
_____	_____
_____	_____

> The local tax assessor's office can provide you with real estate appreciation rates by town, to give you an idea of how in demand certain areas are. Price appreciation reflects the desirability of certain areas, with the home values in sought-after spots increasing more rapidly.

Crime Rate

Each city and town tracks its own crime statistics, which you can most easily obtain by asking the local police department. Find out what the area crime rate is for violent and property crime to determine how safe you would feel living there.

What are the current crime rates?		
City	Violent Crime	Property Crime
_____	_____	_____
_____	_____	_____
_____	_____	_____
_____	_____	_____
_____	_____	_____
_____	_____	_____

According to a 2007 article in *Entrepreneur* magazine, researchers have found a correlation between crime and property values. One source, using crime, property, and rent data from Chicago, found that a 10.0 percent decrease in crime tends to increase property values by between 2.0 and 4.5 percent. Another found aggregate property values suffered as crime rates increased.

Amenities

Some areas have services and amenities that are available, or perhaps available free of charge, only to local residents. In some cases, these freebies have been enough to sway purchasers. What are some of the amenities that towns in your area offer?

What bonus municipal services are offered in your town?

Amenity	Town
Day-care center	_____
Dump/recycling facility	_____
Garbage pick-up	_____
Golf course	_____
Library	_____
Low-cost municipal power	_____
Meeting/conference space	_____
Playground	_____
Recreation center	_____
Shuttle service	_____
Snowplowing	_____
Swimming pool	_____
Other	_____
Other	_____
Other	_____

Environmental Eyesores

Although not necessarily hazardous, some environmental features, such as dumps, power lines, and industrial plants, may affect the value of properties in close proximity. Some you may not care about and others you may be dead-set against. To help your agent find properties that fit your criteria, decide which of the following environmental features or services you can and can't live with:

What can you live with?

- ☐ Municipal dump/landfill
- ☐ Overhead power lines
- ☐ Power plant
- ☐ Processing plant
- ☐ Refuse incinerator
- ☐ Site of a former industrial operation
- ☐ Underground storage tanks
- ☐ Vacant buildings
- ☐ Vacant lots
- ☐ Other _____
- ☐ Other _____
- ☐ Other _____

Distance from Work

For many buyers, being able to get to work relatively quickly and easily is important, to avoid spending hours on the road every day. How far away are you willing to live, in terms of time or mileage?

How far are you willing to commute?

- ☐ Less than 1 mile
- ☐ 1–5 miles
- ☐ 6–10 miles
- ☐ 11–20 miles
- ☐ More than 20 miles

There is no right or wrong area, it just depends how much time you're willing to spend in transit every morning and evening. However, if you work from home, this may not be a consideration.

Questions to Ask Your Mortgage Broker/Real Estate Agent

Which towns are the most sought-after in this area?

_____

Which towns have seen the greatest real estate price appreciation in the last couple of years?

_____

Which towns do you anticipate will see significant price appreciation within the next five years?

_____

What do you base that belief on? Housing growth? Commercial growth?

_____

Which areas are struggling at the moment?

_____

Which areas do you think I should concentrate on as I start my home search?

_____

Are there any known controversies or issues I should be aware of in those locations, such as a throughway being developed in the next five years?

_____

Notes/Observations

_____

_____

_____

_____

_____

_____

_____

_____

_____

_____

_____

_____

_____

_____

_____

_____

_____

_____

_____

_____

_____

_____

Scoping Out Neighborhoods

In This Chapter

- Locating your perfect zip code
- Picking your neighbors
- Weighing school systems
- Evaluating homeowner rules

It has often been said that choosing your neighborhood—the type, size, location, and people who live in it—is more important than the specific home you select. That's because the homes and people around you will likely have a bigger impact on the value of your investment—your home's appreciation—and your lifestyle than the walls that you live behind.

So what does that mean for you? Only that you should look beyond your own front door. Study the community. Ask a lot of questions of your real estate agent and people who currently live in the neighborhood. What do they like best about the area? What do they like least? If they could choose all over again, would they still opt to live there?

Listen carefully to what they tell you, to help you decide whether this is the kind of neighborhood you've been searching for.

The Neighborhood

As you start touring residential areas, think about what kind of homes you'd like to have around your own. Older? Newer? Diverse? Urban?

What kind of neighborhood do you want?

M = Must have
N = Nice to have
U = Unnecessary

_____	Older homes
_____	Part of a newer tract
_____	Part of a development
_____	Gated community/doorman building
_____	Mix of residential and commercial
_____	Solely residential
_____	Appreciating home values
_____	Streetlights
_____	Sidewalks
_____	Little traffic
_____	Low ambient noise
_____	Active homeowners association
_____	Neighborhood restrictions
_____	Low crime rate
_____	Parking accessible
_____	Mature trees

_____   Ample distance between homes

_____   Access to local pool club

_____   Snow removal provided

_____   Garbage pickup provided

_____   Leaf-cleaning provided

The local police department is a great source of information about the various neighborhoods in your area. The public information officer should be able to provide you with crime statistics for the area, and may even be able to localize it by street or block.

Size

Neighborhoods are often bounded by major streets, defined by a development name or part of town, or associated with a particular landmark, such as a park or lake.

How big do you want your neighborhood?

☐ Fewer than 50 properties or units

☐ 51–100 properties

☐ 101–150 properties

☐ 151–200 properties

☐ 201–250 properties

☐ 251–300 properties

☐ More than 300 properties

> Resale-wise, the best home to own within a neighborhood is the one located right in the middle. Being on the edges is not as solid as being surrounded by other neighborhood properties. It's also best to find a neighborhood with similar size and style homes—they don't need to be exactly alike, but the more homogeneous, the better for your resale potential later. (You don't want to own the largest, most expensive home in the neighborhood.)

Location

By now you've probably started forming opinions about different areas in and around your city or town. Let's get them down on paper. What are your preferences thus far?

Where do you want your neighborhood?
☐ East side of the city
☐ West side of the city
☐ North of the city
☐ South of the city
☐ Right downtown
☐ Just outside the downtown area
☐ Suburbia
☐ Other _____

The more detailed you can be about your preferences, the easier it will be to find the home that is meant for you.

Character/Reputation

The more well defined a neighborhood's edges, the more likely it has its own vibe or character. What kind of neighborhood character are you after?

Check all the words that describe your ideal neighborhood.

What's the neighborhood like?
☐ Hip
☐ Funky
☐ Edgy
☐ Artsy
☐ Upscale
☐ Up and coming
☐ Mature
☐ Quiet
☐ Cozy
☐ Friendly
☐ Wild
☐ Involved
☐ Tony/expensive
☐ Young
☐ Private
☐ Pristine
☐ Eclectic
☐ Other _____

Take a look at your preferred words and share them with your agent so that he or she can match your interests with the local communities.

> Neighborhoods are either improving, declining, or stable in terms of livability. See whether you can categorize the neighborhoods you are considering. It's much better to buy into an up-and-coming area than into one that is struggling or declining.

Transportation and Parking

Access to parking may be a major factor in your home search, especially if you live within the city limits.

What are your parking requirements?

- ☐ Enclosed attached garage
- ☐ Enclosed detached garage
- ☐ Carport
- ☐ Driveway
- ☐ On-street parking
- ☐ Designated parking spot
- ☐ Nearby parking garage
- ☐ Other _____

The availability of parking can significantly affect the value of your home. The value of parking spaces alone have been increasing 13 to 20 percent a year, says Stephen Sinclair of Parkingsearch.com. Be mindful of this as you evaluate homes and condos that may not come with parking.

Association/Neighborhood Rules

Some neighborhoods have formal or informal associations that guide the overall functioning of the area. Some focus on safety, perhaps organizing a neighborhood watch program, while others go beyond safety to include rules about aesthetics. Find out up front what kind of neighborhood rules, if any, you'd need to live by.

Which neighborhood has which rules?		
Neighborhood #1	#2	#3
Laundry not permitted to be hung out to dry on a clothesline ☐	☐	☐
Specific mailbox to be used ☐	☐	☐
No extra cars in driveway ☐	☐	☐
No RVs or trailers left in driveway ☐	☐	☐
No above-ground pool (in-ground only) ☐	☐	☐
No outdoor wood storage ☐	☐	☐
Nothing left on front lawn ☐	☐	☐
Grass height not to exceed a certain level ☐	☐	☐
Limitations on pets ☐	☐	☐

continues

Which neighborhood has which rules? (continued)

	Neighborhood #1	#2	#3
Particular trees/plants specified for landscaping	☐	☐	☐
Limitations on lighting	☐	☐	☐
House color limited to specific paint shades	☐	☐	☐
No loud noises after a certain hour	☐	☐	☐
Flags permitted outside the home	☐	☐	☐
Limitations on types of holiday décor	☐	☐	☐
Limitations on length of time holiday décor can be displayed	☐	☐	☐
Limitations on color of interior drapes	☐	☐	☐

Take a look at each neighborhood to assess which is the most and least restrictive. Then decide which of the rules you are and aren't willing to abide by—that will help narrow your choices.

Although generally very difficult to get until you are a member of the homeowners association, ask for or try to borrow a copy of the association's covenants, conditions, and restrictions (CC&Rs) document. By skimming it, you may be able to pick out some of the big restrictions you'll need to be willing to live with.

The Community

Are you looking for small-town living, suburbia, or downtown activity in your next domain? Rate each site on how important it is that your new home be close to each of the following:

What is your community wishlist?

M = Must have
N = Nice to have
U = Unnecessary

_____	Family members
_____	Friends
_____	Highways
_____	Subway/bus
_____	Airport
_____	Work
_____	Volunteer causes
_____	Hospital
_____	Doctors' offices
_____	School
_____	Day care
_____	Church/temple
_____	Grocery store
_____	Shopping
_____	Library
_____	Health club
_____	Sports fields/courts
_____	Golf courses

continues

What is your community wishlist? (continued)
_____ Parks/waterfront
_____ Restaurants/nightclubs
_____ Theater/music venues
_____ Other _____

> The Community Association Institute reports that approximately one in six Americans lives in a community governed by a homeowners association. Four out of five houses built since the late 1990s are part of a homeowners association.

The Schools

For young families, sometimes the school district is the driving factor in selecting an area in which to live. If this applies to your family, what type of school are you seeking?

What kind of school district are you looking for?
M = Must have
N = Nice to have
U = Unnecessary
_____ Large district
_____ Small district
_____ Many schools
_____ Few schools
_____ Newer facilities
_____ Top state report card grade

_____	Superintendent longevity
_____	Low teacher turnover
_____	Solid reputation
_____	Strong leadership
_____	Rigorous curriculum
_____	Experienced teachers
_____	Small class size
_____	Busing available
_____	Sports programs available
_____	Arts and music available
_____	Award-winning
_____	Special needs accommodations
_____	Responsive to inquiries
_____	Up-to-date technology
_____	School choice program in place
_____	Other _____

Now that you have a list of features that describe the school you'd most like your children to attend, it's time to evaluate the one(s) that serve your neighborhood.

What is offered by the school that your child would attend?

_____	Number of students
_____	Student-teacher ratio
_____	Open campus policy
_____	Enrichment programs

continues

What is offered by the school that your child would attend? (continued)

_____ After-school care

_____ After-school activities

_____ Special education available

_____ Strong athletic program

_____ Strong arts program

_____ Community service requirement

_____ International Baccalaureate available

_____ Regent's diploma available

_____ Advanced Placement courses available

_____ Honors program available

_____ Short bus commute

_____ College prep program

_____ Personalized report cards

_____ Uniform requirement

_____ Breakfast programs

_____ Morning bus availability

_____ Late bus availability

_____ Student safety

_____ Withdrawal policy

_____ College attendance rate

How does the school stack up? Is it time to look in a different neighborhood, or have you just confirmed that this is the community for you?

Even if you aren't concerned about the local schools for *your* children, it's smart to investigate their quality to gauge the home's resale potential. Homes in areas with better-performing schools are easier to (re)sell.

The Neighbors

Just as important—maybe more so—as finding a home you love is finding neighbors with whom you can get along. Don't expect to become best friends, although you may, but think about what kind of community you want to become part of.

What kinds of words would you like to describe your new neighborhood?

M = Must have
N = Nice to have
U = Unnecessary

_____	Close-knit community
_____	Residents your age
_____	A mixture of ages
_____	Stay-at-home parents common
_____	Older couples
_____	Dual-income couples
_____	Gay/Lesbian-friendly
_____	Supportive of a neighborhood watch program
_____	Primarily resident owners, not renters
_____	College students

continues

What kinds of words would you like to describe your new neighborhood? (continued)

_____ Corporate executives

_____ Other _____

> Although you may try and pump your real estate agent for information about a particular neighborhood, such as the age of the residents or the quality of the school system, he or she is not permitted to tell you. To get the information you want, spend some time scoping out the neighborhood yourself.

Questions to Ask Your Mortgage Broker/Real Estate Agent

Which neighborhoods in the area are stable or up and coming?

_____

_____

Which neighborhoods are likely to have all the features and amenities I'm looking for, based on my checklist?

_____

_____

Which neighborhoods have a shortage of available parking?

_____

_____

Are any neighborhood associations known to have a more restrictive CC&R document?

_____

_____

Are there any neighborhoods with amenities I should pay close attention to, such as a pool or rec center, for example?

_____

_____

Are there any neighborhoods I should steer clear of, in your opinion?

_____

_____

What would your top three neighborhood recommendations be, given what I've told you I'm looking for?

_____

_____

Which districts have received the most honors or awards in recent years?

_____

_____

Are there any on state warning lists?

_____

_____

Which school would my children attend based on the neighborhoods I'm looking at or that you've recommended?

_____

_____

Are there any downsides to those neighborhoods?

_____

_____

Notes/Observations

_____

_____

_____

_____

_____

_____

_____

_____

_____

_____

_____

_____

_____

_____

_____

_____

_____

_____

_____

_____

_____

Your Dream Home

In this Chapter

- Zeroing in on your perfect home
- Defining your likes and dislikes
- Defining must-haves and nice-to-haves
- Setting priorities

Before you start scheduling home tours, decide first what features are most important to you in your new home. Do you want to be in the city or do you have to have lots of land? Are you after a one-level condo or would a multi-story townhouse do? What's the minimum number of bedrooms you require? How about the number of bathrooms? Which features are critical and which are not?

You'll save yourself time and aggravation, and increase your odds of finding your dream home in no time, by first completing this chapter's checklists and forms. You may even discover some priorities you didn't know you had.

Type of Home

Beware of setting a hard-and-fast maximum asking price you'll consider. You may end up excluding several homes that would be perfect and would be within your budget. That's because in most cases, you'll be able to negotiate a purchase price that is lower—even far lower—than the asking price. Be a little flexible in the prices of homes you tour.

So what kind of home are you after? Check the types of structures you would consider:

Do you want a single-family house or condo?
☐ Condominium
☐ Coop
☐ Townhouse
☐ Single-family home
☐ Duplex
☐ Multifamily property

Although you may think that condominiums, coops (or cooperatives), and townhouses are much the same, in terms of ownership rights, they're not. Condominiums and townhouses provide for individual ownership of the real estate inside the living structure, while coops provide factional ownership of an entire building with a lease to a particular unit.

Style of Home

If you've decided a single family home will best suit your needs, you may be surprised to learn that there are many different architectural formats to choose from. The main difference in each is the placement of the staircase relative to the front door. Which layout might work for you?

Cape or Dutch Colonial?

- ☐ Bungalow: Low roof, pillared front door
- ☐ Cape/Cape Cod: Central door and staircase
- ☐ Colonial: Symmetrical shape, central doorway
- ☐ Contemporary: Modern clean lines
- ☐ Duplex: Side-by-side, two-family home
- ☐ Dutch colonial: Broad roof mimics a barn
- ☐ Federal: Low-pitched roof, narrow side windows
- ☐ French Provincial: High-pitched roof, symmetry
- ☐ Georgian: Symmetrical design
- ☐ Gothic Revival: Details inspired by churches
- ☐ Greek Revival: Front pillars
- ☐ Italianate: Victorian
- ☐ Neoclassical: Reminiscent of ancient Greece and Rome
- ☐ Pueblo: Southwestern desert style
- ☐ Ranch: Single story
- ☐ Second Empire: Tall with wrought ironwork
- ☐ Split-level: Half-stories up and down

continues

Cape or Dutch Colonial? (continued)

□ Tidewater: Wrap-around porches, common on the coast

□ Tudor: Angular lines and decorative exterior trim

Knowing a few home-style terms can help you define what you're looking for to your real estate agent. If you don't like symmetry, you'll want to look beyond Capes and Colonials, for example.

Age of Home

In general, the newer the home, the higher the cost per square foot you'll pay to buy it. However, the appliances are often more current; the heating, ventilation, and air conditioning (HVAC) is more likely to be up to date; and less maintenance is typically required. But then, newer homes also don't have the charm and personality of homes from earlier eras. It's a trade-off.

How new do you need?

□ To-be-built

□ Newer (built within last 10 years)

□ Traditional (10–50 years old)

□ Vintage (More than 50 years old)

Sun Exposure

Feng Shui devotees, as well as artists, have very specific preferences regarding the direction their home faces. Depending on your interests, and your plans for use of your yard, sun exposure may or may not play a major role in selecting your home.

Which direction do you want your home to face?
☐ North/northeast
☐ North/northwest
☐ South/southeast
☐ South/southwest

The Home's Exterior

There's an old saying that the exterior of a home is much more expensive to change than the interior, so make sure you like the exterior first.

What exterior finishes would you consider?
☐ Brick
☐ Brick and siding
☐ Log
☐ Siding—aluminum
☐ Siding—wood
☐ Siding—clapboard
☐ Siding—vinyl

continues

What exterior finishes would you consider? (continued)

- ☐ Stone
- ☐ Stucco
- ☐ Tile roof
- ☐ Slate roof
- ☐ Asphalt shingle roof
- ☐ Front-facing entrance
- ☐ Side-facing entrance
- ☐ Wrap-around front porch
- ☐ Balcony

The materials used on a home's exterior, such as brick or siding, affect the building's appearance and long-term maintenance costs. A slate roof may be stunning, but the cost to repair or replace it may be equally stunning—to your wallet. Likewise, you may love wood siding, but you may not love repainting it every few years. Think about what that exterior will mean in terms of work before committing yourself.

Parking

With the majority of Americans today owning a car, overnight parking near home is an important issue.

What are your parking requirements?

- ☐ Attached garage
- ☐ Semidetached (with a lanai)

☐ Unattached garage, but on property

☐ Carport

☐ Designated parking space

☐ Spot in adjacent lot or garage

☐ One-car garage

☐ Two-car garage

☐ Three-car garage

☐ Front-load garage

☐ Side-load garage

The Yard

Whether you live in a warm climate or cold, during at least part of the year you may want to spend time outdoors. What kind of outdoor space are you after?

What kind of front yard do you need?		
	M = Must have	
	N = Nice to have	
	U = Unnecessary	
_____	None—no grass	
_____	Minimal	
_____	A lot—home is set back from street	
_____	Professionally landscaped	
_____	Tree-filled	
_____	Zeroscaped (installing native plants for reduced water consumption)	
_____	Front walkway	

The backyard is often considered more important than the front yard. What kind of backyard do you envision for yourself?

What kind of backyard do you want?

M = Must have
N = Nice to have
U = Unnecessary

_____ Large space

_____ Private

_____ Not shared

_____ Fenced-in

_____ Grassy

_____ Pool

_____ Hot tub

_____ Invisible fence for pets

_____ Sprinkler/irrigation system

_____ Built-in grill/cooking station

_____ Patio

_____ Deck

_____ Mature trees

_____ Garden

_____ Backs to forever wild

_____ Waterfront

Perhaps the most important feature to consider in the backyard is the amount of space available. You can make just about any change—adding a pool, putting in a patio, planting trees and shrubs—but the one thing you can't add easily is land. Make sure what is there will work for you.

Your Home's Interior

You may be able to compromise on a home's exterior, but there are certainly some non-negotiable requirements your new home needs to meet. What are they?

What layout do you want for your home?

M = Must have
N = Nice to have
U = Unnecessary

_____ Open floor plan

_____ Large front foyer

_____ Central staircase

_____ Back staircase

Kitchen

_____ Eat-in

_____ Galley

_____ Kitchen island

_____ Plenty of counter space

_____ Wood cabinets

_____ Gas appliances

continues

What layout do you want for your home? (continued)

_____ Professional grade appliances

_____ Plenty of lighting

_____ Granite/marble counters

Dining room

_____ Formal dining room

_____ Wainscoting

_____ Crown molding

_____ Chandelier

_____ Adjacent to kitchen

_____ Hardwood floors

Living room

_____ Separate formal living room/salon

_____ Hardwood floors

_____ Carpeted floors

_____ Vaulted ceiling

_____ Large windows

_____ Fireplace

_____ Built-in bookcases

Family/great room

_____ Carpeted floors

_____ Hardwood floors

_____ Fireplace

_____ Built-in bookcases

_____ Large windows

_____ Vaulted ceiling

_____ Surround-sound system

Bedrooms

_____ Number needed: _____

_____ Master suite

_____ Walk-in closet

_____ Ceiling fans

Bathrooms

_____ Number of full bathrooms needed: _____

_____ Number of half bathrooms needed: _____

_____ Jacuzzi

_____ Bidet

_____ Separate shower

_____ Multiple showerheads

Laundry

_____ First-floor location

_____ Storage space available

_____ Appliances included

Basement

_____ Finished

_____ Unfinished

_____ Walk-out

_____ Storage area

_____ Additional bedroom(s)

Attic

_____ Storage available

_____ Expansion potential

Additional areas

_____ Home office

_____ Media room

continues

What layout do you want for your home? (continued)

_____	Mudroom
_____	In-law apartment/suite
_____	Bonus room

Other amenities

_____	Handicap accessible
_____	Blinds/window treatments
_____	Skylights
_____	Security system

> Rooms that have closets and modes of entry and exit (a window or door) are officially classified as bedrooms. Since you'll pay more for an extra bedroom, both in the purchase price and in property taxes, make sure you will actually use it as such. If you can't fit a bed in, or it's in the back of the basement, do you really want to pay extra for it?

Infrastructure

Your new home's look is important, but how it was designed to function can have an even bigger impact on your wallet.

What are your preferences utility-wise?

M = Must have
N = Nice to have
U = Unnecessary

_____ Gas heat

_____ Electric heat

_____ Oil heat

_____ Wood-burning stove

_____ Pellet stove

_____ Gas water heater

_____ Electric water heater

_____ Filtered furnace

_____ Central air conditioning

_____ Sewer

_____ Septic system

_____ Connected to city water

_____ Well water

Questions to Ask Your Real Estate Agent

How difficult do you think it will be to find a home with the features we've outlined in this neighborhood?

_____

_____

Would you say that we're in a buyer's market or a seller's market right now?

_____

_____

What does that translate into in terms of a discount I might be able to negotiate or a premium I'll need to pay to get the home I want?

_____

_____

What do you expect I will need to be flexible on?

_____

_____

What do the typical homes in this area have in terms of features?

_____

_____

Notes/Observations

_____
_____
_____
_____
_____
_____
_____
_____
_____
_____
_____
_____
_____
_____
_____
_____
_____
_____
_____
_____
_____
_____

Chapter 5

Contenders

In This Chapter

- Whittling down your list of possibilities
- Weighing pros and cons
- Remaining objective
- Zeroing in on a preferred property

You're getting close. You've found some homes that meet most, if not all, of your needs and it is decision time. Try and put aside any emotional attachments you may have to any of the properties and objectively weigh the advantages and disadvantages of each.

To help you figure out which home will best suit you—now and in the future—evaluate all of the homes you are seriously considering according to their value and fit for your lifestyle. Be honest with yourself and your best choice will start to emerge.

Size

The one factor that affects the value of your home perhaps more than any other is its square footage—how much interior living space do you have.

What size home are you aiming for?				
	Home #1	#2	#3	#4
Square footage	_____	_____	_____	_____
Number of bedrooms	_____	_____	_____	_____
Number of bathrooms	_____	_____	_____	_____
Number of stories	_____	_____	_____	_____
Size of garage (# cars)	_____	_____	_____	_____
Size of lot	_____	_____	_____	_____

Although the total size of one home may be larger than another, take note of room sizes, too. If you anticipate spending most of your time in the kitchen or family room and those are the smallest spaces in the home, the actual livable space may be less than what you need.

Type of Construction

Although you may never really notice how the home was built, finding out now can help you evaluate how much upkeep may be needed over the long haul.

What type of construction would you prefer?

Construction	Home #1	#2	#3	#4
Wood	☐	☐	☐	☐
Wood and brick	☐	☐	☐	☐
Brick	☐	☐	☐	☐
Log	☐	☐	☐	☐
Post and beam	☐	☐	☐	☐
Other	☐	☐	☐	☐

Exterior	Home #1	#2	#3	#4
Brick	☐	☐	☐	☐
Brick and siding	☐	☐	☐	☐
Log	☐	☐	☐	☐
Siding—aluminum	☐	☐	☐	☐
Siding—wood	☐	☐	☐	☐
Siding—clapboard	☐	☐	☐	☐
Siding—vinyl	☐	☐	☐	☐
Stone	☐	☐	☐	☐
Stucco	☐	☐	☐	☐

Homes constructed of stone, brick, or stucco are generally considered more desirable than wood-framed homes covered with less expensive siding. However, this need not be a factor in your decision unless the property you're considering is in an area of stone or brick homes and yours is 100 percent siding. If that is the case, just be aware that, all things being equal, your sided home will not be perceived to be as valuable. But if all the homes in the area are sided, you will be in good shape.

Rooms

How many rooms does each home have? Although the square footage of two (or more) homes can be the same, how they are laid out leads to very different uses of space and a different configuration of rooms.

How many rooms does each home have?				
Indoor Layout	Home #1	#2	#3	#4
Foyer	☐	☐	☐	☐
Kitchen	☐	☐	☐	☐
Breakfast room	☐	☐	☐	☐
Pantry	☐	☐	☐	☐
Dining room	☐	☐	☐	☐
Living room	☐	☐	☐	☐
Family room	☐	☐	☐	☐
Great room	☐	☐	☐	☐
Den	☐	☐	☐	☐
Home office	☐	☐	☐	☐
Media room	☐	☐	☐	☐
Laundry	☐	☐	☐	☐
Master bedroom	☐	☐	☐	☐
Guest bedroom	☐	☐	☐	☐
Bedroom #1	☐	☐	☐	☐
Bedroom #2	☐	☐	☐	☐
Bedroom #3	☐	☐	☐	☐
Bedroom #4	☐	☐	☐	☐

Indoor Layout	Home #1	#2	#3	#4
Bedroom #5	☐	☐	☐	☐
Powder room	☐	☐	☐	☐
Bathroom #1	☐	☐	☐	☐
Bathroom #2	☐	☐	☐	☐
Bathroom #3	☐	☐	☐	☐
Bathroom #4	☐	☐	☐	☐
Basement	☐	☐	☐	☐
Finished basement	☐	☐	☐	☐
Attic	☐	☐	☐	☐
In-law suite	☐	☐	☐	☐
Bonus room	☐	☐	☐	☐
Car port	☐	☐	☐	☐
One-car garage	☐	☐	☐	☐
Two-car garage	☐	☐	☐	☐
Three-car garage	☐	☐	☐	☐
Other _____	☐	☐	☐	☐

Your Outdoor Living Space

With the current trend toward more outdoor living, the space available in the front and back yards of the homes you are considering should be given serious thought.

What kind of outdoor space do you seek?

Outdoor Features	Home #1	#2	#3	#4
Front porch	☐	☐	☐	☐
Landscaping	☐	☐	☐	☐
Forever wild backyard	☐	☐	☐	☐
Mature trees	☐	☐	☐	☐
Garden	☐	☐	☐	☐
Deck	☐	☐	☐	☐
Outdoor cooking station	☐	☐	☐	☐
Screen porch	☐	☐	☐	☐
Fenced-in	☐	☐	☐	☐
Patio	☐	☐	☐	☐
Pool	☐	☐	☐	☐
Other _____	☐	☐	☐	☐

Depending on the climate you live in, the amount of yard space a home offers may or may not be a big deal. Also, if the home is near a park, then not having a big yard may not matter at all. Remember—the larger the yard, the more upkeep it will require, too.

Age

A home's age probably won't affect its value much unless it is brand new and buyers are willing to pay a premium for that new carpet smell, or it is very old and needing a lot of work. Do any of your contenders fall into those categories?

How old would you prefer the home to be?				
	Home #1	#2	#3	#4
To-be-built	☐	☐	☐	☐
Newer (less than 10 years)	☐	☐	☐	☐
Traditional (10–50 years old)	☐	☐	☐	☐
Vintage (more than 50 years old)	☐	☐	☐	☐

One thing to be aware of is that a home's property assessment becomes less accurate as the home ages. So the newer the home, the closer the assessment will be to the actual value. The older the home, the more you'll want to rely on comps to ensure you don't overpay.

Amenities

Sometimes what stands out about a home isn't the number of rooms or the type of siding, but a unique or attractive feature.

Are there particular home amenities you're after?				
	Home #1	#2	#3	#4
Fireplace	☐	☐	☐	☐
Wood stove	☐	☐	☐	☐
Gas stove	☐	☐	☐	☐
Hot tub	☐	☐	☐	☐

continues

Are there particular home amenities you're after? (continued)	Home #1	#2	#3	#4
Walk-in closet	☐	☐	☐	☐
First-floor laundry	☐	☐	☐	☐
Second-floor laundry	☐	☐	☐	☐
Elevator	☐	☐	☐	☐
Doorman	☐	☐	☐	☐
Balcony	☐	☐	☐	☐
Skylights	☐	☐	☐	☐
Lawn irrigation system	☐	☐	☐	☐
Outdoor fountain	☐	☐	☐	☐
Other _____	☐	☐	☐	☐

Although a particular amenity may be pushing you to pay top dollar for a home you love, take a step back and determine how much it would cost to add that same feature to a lower-priced property. Why pay an extra $8,000 for a home with a gas stove, for example, when you can buy a new stove for $4,000 and install it wherever you want?

Noise

You probably don't think much about the sounds you hear near your current home, but before you commit yourself to spending many years surrounded by loud or irritating noises, visit the different homes at various times of the day. A property may be perfect during the day but downright noisy when kids get out of school, for example. Know before you buy.

How noisy are the neighborhoods you're looking at?				
Quiet Hours	Home #1	#2	#3	#4
Early morning	☐	☐	☐	☐
Lunch hour	☐	☐	☐	☐
Afternoon	☐	☐	☐	☐
Early evening	☐	☐	☐	☐
Nighttime	☐	☐	☐	☐
After midnight	☐	☐	☐	☐

> Be suspicious if a home is available for show only at certain hours. On a recent HGTV show, a real estate agent told of a case where a buyer was interested in a home that he was allowed to view only between 9:00 and 10:00 in the morning. As it turned out, during other hours of the day, an extremely loud train whistle could be heard as the train barreled by the home. Unless the buyer had taken the time to check the home out at different hours, he wouldn't have known until it was too late.

Condition

Every home has minor items that need touching up, from paint to small nicks in doors to tile that needs recaulking. These are minor repairs. Keep an eye out for larger issues that could be costly and time consuming.

How much renovating does each home need?				
	Home #1	#2	#3	#4
Exterior	___	___	___	___
Roof	___	___	___	___
Garage	___	___	___	___
Foundation	___	___	___	___
Electrical wiring	___	___	___	___
Plumbing	___	___	___	___
Windows	___	___	___	___
Flooring	___	___	___	___
Furnace	___	___	___	___
Water heater	___	___	___	___
Kitchen appliances	___	___	___	___
Other ___	___	___	___	___

Don't worry too much about finding hidden problems yourself—before you finalize the home's purchase, make sure you arrange to have a professional home inspector go through the home from top to bottom. Although you may not be able to spot a damp basement or fraying electrical wires, your inspector can and will.

Timing

The more flexible you can be in your timing,
the better the deal you may be able to negotiate.
However, if you need to be moved in by a certain
date, perhaps because of school or a new job starting, you'll want to keep that in mind as you compare your top choices.

How quickly would you like to move?				
When Can I Move In?	Home #1	#2	#3	#4
Right away	___	___	___	___
Your preferred closing date	___	___	___	___
The earliest that the home is available for closing	___	___	___	___
Deadline for closing (if applicable)	___	___	___	___

Many homes come on the market in the spring in
the hopes that they will sell during the summer
and the seller can get settled in a new home
before the school year starts. This is the busiest
time of year for real estate and when you're likely
to have the largest selection. However, you may
have less competition from other buyers during the
other times of the year.

Homeowner Fees

In addition to being able to enjoy a living space that is all yours, you may also incur some costs you may not be used to paying. One of those could be a condo, coop, or homeowners association fee. You'll want to find out about these charges so you can factor them into your best offer.

What homeowner fees are involved?				
	Home #1	#2	#3	#4
Homeowner association dues	___	___	___	___
Condo association fees	___	___	___	___
Coop fees	___	___	___	___
Assessments	___	___	___	___
Parking fees (if applicable)	___	___	___	___
Pool association fees	___	___	___	___
Other ___	___	___	___	___

Utility Costs

If you've been paying your utilities while renting, you're certainly used to shelling out cash every month for the basics of heat, water, and trash removal, but depending on the size of your space, you may find a big jump in your bills once you're in your own place. Compare the costs of each possible property to help in budgeting, and to spot any less-than-energy-efficient appliances or areas where the insulation is lacking.

What are the different utility costs?				
	Home #1	#2	#3	#4
Electric bill	___	___	___	___
Gas bill	___	___	___	___
Oil bill	___	___	___	___
Water bill	___	___	___	___
Sewer charge	___	___	___	___
Septic charge	___	___	___	___
Garbage collection bill	___	___	___	___
Recycling service bill	___	___	___	___

Make sure you're comparing apples to apples when examining utility costs across the homes you're considering. If a property has been vacant for more than a week or so, its utility bill will be unusually low and you'll want to take that into account. An empty home's gas or oil bill will be dramatically lower than if someone were living there.

Taxes

The good news about property taxes is that they're fully deductible on your tax reporting. The bad news is that you have to pay them in the first place, but at least you get a credit for having done so.

What are the taxes on each home?				
	Home #1	#2	#3	#4
Property taxes	___	___	___	___
School taxes	___	___	___	___
City taxes	___	___	___	___

> Keep in mind that as soon as you close on the sale of your new home, you can petition for a lower property tax valuation if you buy for less than the assessed value. That's because assessments are based on the estimated value, but market value—what is actually paid for a home—trumps estimates, and you can almost always have your assessment lowered. If you pay more than the assessment, however, you may not want to rush to report it. The assessors will find out soon enough.

School District

Buyers with school-age children are likely to be more concerned about the quality and size of the local school than other buyers. However, because the desirability of the local school district affects the value of homes within the district, all prospective home buyers should check out the district's school system. Use a + or - to indicate a district's relative strengths:

What kind of school district do you want?

	Home #1	#2	#3	#4
Number of students	____	____	____	____
Number of schools	____	____	____	____
Student/teacher ratio	____	____	____	____
Test scores	____	____	____	____
Availability of special education	____	____	____	____
Availability of enrichment	____	____	____	____
Availability of AP courses	____	____	____	____
Percent graduating	____	____	____	____
Percent attending college	____	____	____	____
Reputation	____	____	____	____

If you love a particular house, but aren't enthused by the school district, find out whether your area offers school choice. An increasing number of districts are permitting families to choose which school their child will attend rather than requiring that they stay within their district of residence. And in that case, the district you live in may be less of an issue.

Distance from Work

To avoid spending hours each workday on the road traveling to and from work, time how long a round-trip commute takes from each home. You may discover that commuting to and from a home that is farther away actually takes less time, given the route you would take. It is better to know that now rather than later, as you sit in traffic.

How far is each home from work?				
	Home #1	#2	#3	#4
Miles to work	___	___	___	___
Morning commute (minutes)	___	___	___	___
Evening commute (minutes)	___	___	___	___

One possible way to avoid driving during the most traffic-infested hours of the day is to ask your employer about flextime. It doesn't work for everyone, but many employees find that being able to start work before the morning rush hour and end before the typical evening commute begins saves them considerable time. Shifting your route or your drive time can open your home options even further.

Value/Cost

Another useful way to compare homes is by looking at their cost per square foot. Make sure you compare them to your comparables as well, to see whether there are any bargains to be had or if any are overpriced.

What is the cost-to-value ratio for each home?				
	Home #1	#2	#3	#4
Asking price	___	___	___	___
÷ Square footage	___	___	___	___
= Cost per square foot	___	___	___	___

Questions to Ask Your Mortgage Broker/Real Estate Agent

Which of these homes has the greatest potential for appreciation in the next five years and why?

_____

_____

Which one has the least potential for appreciation and why?

_____

_____

Which one(s) would be most difficult to resell and why?

_____

_____

What is a typical cost per square foot for homes like these?

_____

_____

Will I have any trouble getting an appraisal at or above the asking price for any of these homes (as a lower appraisal would make getting a mortgage difficult)?

_____

_____

Notes/Observations

Chapter 6

Local Comparables

In This Chapter

- Defining comparables
- Comparing properties
- Calculating cost per square foot
- Strategizing offer price

Once you reach this stage in your home search, you've identified one or more properties that meet all your needs. And while you've confirmed with your agent that the home is within your price range, you probably want to confirm that it is not overpriced. If you pay too much for a home, you will find it much more difficult to sell it at a profit in the future.

Your goal is to pay as little as possible while still being taken seriously by the sellers, so you need to research what similar homes in the area have sold for recently. This process is referred to as looking at local comparables—"comps" for short.

Knowing what similar homes have sold for will (a) reassure you that the asking price is reasonable or (b) give you sound reasoning to offer less. In addition, checking out comparables will help you compare homes to each other. Here are some checklists and forms for tracking the different properties.

Hot Property

Starting with your favorite property so far, let's compare it head to head with up to three recent comps to see how it stacks up price-wise.

How does your favorite home stack up?	
Location	_____
Asking price	_____
Property taxes	_____
Utilities	_____
Fees	_____
School district	_____
Size (sq. ft.)	_____
Type of structure (condo, house, etc.)	_____
Style (Cape, Colonial, etc.)	_____
Age	_____
Condition (excellent, average, poor)	_____
Orientation	_____
Number of bedrooms	_____
Number of bathrooms	_____
Exterior (siding, brick, etc.)	_____

Parking (garage, off-street, etc.) _____

Front yard (large, small, etc.) _____

Backyard (fenced in, spacious, etc.) _____

Layout (open, central staircase, etc.) _____

Kitchen (galley, updated, etc.) _____

Dining room (formal, small, etc.) _____

Living room (formal, not applicable, etc.) _____

Family room (fireplace, not applicable, etc.) _____

Laundry room (basement, first floor, etc.) _____

Basement (finished, walk-out, etc.) _____

Attic (crawl space, finished, etc.) _____

Other rooms

_____ _____

Heating system (gas, electric, oil) _____

Central air conditioning (yes/no) _____

Additional comments_____

_____

_____

Try hard not to fall in love with a home. Yes, it will play a big role in your life for the next few years, but it's also an investment and if you view it as more than that, you're at a disadvantage at the negotiating table. When you fall in love, you're more likely to pay more to have it. Just as there are plenty of other fish in the sea, there are hundreds of other homes on the market, too.

Financial Stats

Before you scan the comps that you've had your
real estate agent gather for you or that you've
researched on your own, run some quick numbers
to see how expensive your favorite home is. One
quick-and-dirty number to look at is the cost per
square foot, which you can easily compare to any
other property, no matter the size.

What is the home's cost per square foot?	
Property location	_____
Asking price	_____
÷ Size in square feet	_____
= Cost per square foot	_____

Armed with this information, study up to three
homes—or more if you can find them—that are
very similar in location, size, number of bedrooms
and bathrooms, and condition.

The Comparables

Just as you broke down the specific features of the
home you are considering for purchase, take careful
note of the features of comparable homes. These
will give you an idea of how your favorite stacks up.

How does comparable #1 stack up?

Location	_____
Asking price	_____
Property taxes	_____
Utilities	_____
Fees	_____
School district	_____
Size (sq. ft.)	_____
Type of structure (condo, house, etc.)	_____
Style (Cape, Colonial, etc.)	_____
Age	_____
Condition (excellent, average, poor)	_____
Orientation	_____
Number of bedrooms	_____
Number of bathrooms	_____
Exterior (siding, brick, etc.)	_____
Parking (garage, off-street, etc.)	_____
Front yard (large, small, etc.)	_____
Backyard (fenced in, spacious, etc.)	_____
Layout (open, central staircase, etc.)	_____
Kitchen (galley, updated, etc.)	_____
Dining room (formal, small, etc.)	_____
Living room (formal, not applicable, etc.)	_____
Family room (fireplace, not applicable, etc.)	_____
Laundry room (basement, first floor, etc.)	_____

continues

How does comparable #1 stack up? (continued)

Basement (finished, walk-out, etc.)   _____

Attic (crawl space, finished, etc.)   _____

Other rooms

_____   _____

Heating system (gas, electric, oil)   _____

Central air conditioning (yes/no)   _____

Additional comments_____

_____

_____

What is comparable #1's cost per square foot?

Property location   _____

Asking price   _____

÷ Size in square feet   _____

= Cost per square foot   _____

Limit your list of comparables to properties that have sold within the last three months, but not earlier. With the quickly shifting real estate market today, a home that sold six or nine months ago was not facing the same conditions as last month and should be disregarded. That property is not a fair comparison.

How does comparable #2 stack up?

Location	_____
Asking price	_____
Property taxes	_____
Utilities	_____
Fees	_____
School district	_____
Size (sq. ft.)	_____
Type of structure (condo, house, etc.)	_____
Style (Cape, Colonial, etc.)	_____
Age	_____
Condition (excellent, average, poor)	_____
Orientation	_____
Number of bedrooms	_____
Number of bathrooms	_____
Exterior (siding, brick, etc.)	_____
Parking (garage, off-street, etc.)	_____
Front yard (large, small, etc.)	_____
Backyard (fenced in, spacious, etc.)	_____
Layout (open, central staircase, etc.)	_____
Kitchen (galley, updated, etc.)	_____
Dining room (formal, small, etc.)	_____
Living room (formal, not applicable, etc.)	_____
Family room (fireplace, not applicable, etc.)	_____
Laundry room (basement, first floor, etc.)	_____

continues

How does comparable #2 stack up? (continued)

Basement (finished, walk-out, etc.) _____

Attic (crawl space, finished, etc.) _____

Other rooms

_____ _____

Heating system (gas, electric, oil) _____

Central air conditioning (yes/no) _____

Additional comments_____

_____

_____

What is comparable #2's cost per square foot?

Property location _____

Asking price _____

÷ Size in square feet _____

= Cost per square foot _____

Beyond looking at homes that have sold in the area, it's interesting to compare what builders are charging per square foot for new homes. If you're buying an existing home of a similar size and location as a new home, you should expect to pay less per square foot.

How does comparable #3 stack up?

Location _____

Asking price _____

Property taxes _____

Utilities _____

Fees _____

School district _____

Size (sq. ft.) _____

Type of structure (condo, house, etc.) _____

Style (Cape, Colonial, etc.) _____

Age _____

Condition (excellent, average, poor) _____

Orientation _____

Number of bedrooms _____

Number of bathrooms _____

Exterior (siding, brick, etc.) _____

Parking (garage, off-street, etc.) _____

Front yard (large, small, etc.) _____

Backyard (fenced in, spacious, etc.) _____

Layout (open, central staircase, etc.) _____

Kitchen (galley, updated, etc.) _____

Dining room (formal, small, etc.) _____

Living room (formal, not applicable, etc.) _____

Family room (fireplace, not applicable, etc.) _____

Laundry room (basement, first floor, etc.) _____

continues

How does comparable #3 stack up? (continued)

Basement (finished, walk-out, etc.)   _____

Attic (crawl space, finished, etc.)   _____

Other rooms

_____   _____

Heating system (gas, electric, oil)   _____

Central air conditioning (yes/no)   _____

Additional comments_____

_____

_____

What is comparable #3's cost per square foot?

Property location   _____

Asking price   _____

÷ Size in square feet   _____

= Cost per square foot   _____

Sometimes the little things can have a big impact on asking price. Look carefully at the brand of kitchen appliances or the type of flooring. Even the amount and quality of landscaping can push a price up above that of neighboring homes. Keep an eye out for upgrades that might explain a higher-than-average asking price.

Pros and Cons

Although price is one major factor to consider when buying your first home, sometimes it can help to do a head-to-head comparison to see more clearly your favorite home's pluses and minuses.

Comparing your prospective home to the three comparables, give the comps a plus (+) or a minus (-) depending on how they stack up.

How do your comps' features compare head to head?			
Features	#1	#2	#3
Location	___	___	___
Asking price	___	___	___
Property taxes	___	___	___
Utilities	___	___	___
Fees	___	___	___
School district	___	___	___
Size (sq. ft.)	___	___	___
Type of structure (condo, house, etc.)	___	___	___
Style (Cape, Colonial, etc.)	___	___	___
Age	___	___	___
Condition (excellent, average, poor)	___	___	___
Orientation	___	___	___
Number of bedrooms	___	___	___
Number of bathrooms	___	___	___
Exterior (siding, brick, etc.)	___	___	___

continues

How do your comps' features compare head to head? (continued)			
Features	#1	#2	#3
Parking (garage, off-street, etc.)	___	___	___
Front yard (large, small, etc.)	___	___	___
Backyard (fenced in, spacious, etc.)	___	___	___
Layout (open, central staircase, etc.)	___	___	___
Kitchen (galley, updated, etc.)	___	___	___
Dining room (formal, small, etc.)	___	___	___
Living room (formal, not applicable, etc.)	___	___	___
Family room (fireplace, not applicable, etc.)	___	___	___
Laundry room (basement, first floor, etc.)	___	___	___
Basement (finished, walk-out, etc.)	___	___	___
Attic (crawl space, finished, etc.)	___	___	___
Other rooms	___	___	___
Heating system (gas, electric, oil)	___	___	___
Central air conditioning (yes/no)	___	___	___
Additional comments_____			

Rather than evaluating a home's price as a stand-alone figure, look at the price of homes in the immediate area. In a perfect world, the home you're interested in should be the average of the other homes, or lower. The reason? The lower the comparative price, the more price appreciation potential you have.

Selling Price

As you start zeroing in on an appropriate price for your favorite home, your next question may be, "What should I offer?" And again, those comps can be your guide.

Take a look at what percent of the asking price the homes sold for, which should give you a general idea of where to start with your first offer. (You may want to have a calculator handy.)

How much of a discount was there on the asking price?			
	#1	#2	#3
Asking price	_____	_____	_____
- Selling price	_____	_____	_____
= Difference	_____	_____	_____
÷ Asking price	_____	_____	_____
= Discount taken	_____	_____	_____

Depending on how varied the discounts off the asking price are, you may want to take an average of the comparable discounts to come up with a target price you want to pay for your favorite home.

Don't start at this price, however, because this is where you want to end up in your negotiations, not necessarily where you want to start. The only reason to start high with your offer is if you are in a strong real estate market or if there are competing offers on the table. Ask your realtor for advice in this situation.

Questions to Ask Your Mortgage Broker/Real Estate Agent

Based on your experience, are the homes I'm looking at priced appropriately?

_____

_____

Which of the comparables you've shown me most closely matches my favorite home?

_____

_____

What factors affect asking prices in this area?

_____

_____

What is an appropriate cost per square foot for the area I'm looking at?

_____

_____

Are there any features in the home I like that put it at a disadvantage for resale (such as a pool or lack of a fireplace)?

_____

_____

Would you anticipate any problems getting an appraisal for the asking price, should I decide to make an offer?

_____

_____

Have any offers been made on this home in the past few months?

_____

_____

What were they?

_____

_____

Why were they turned down?

_____

_____

What is the minimum the seller is looking to get out of this sale?

_____

_____

Notes/Observations

_____

_____

_____

_____

_____

_____

_____

_____

_____

_____

_____

_____

_____

_____

_____

_____

_____

_____

_____

_____

Chapter 7

Digging for Answers

In This Chapter

- Researching details
- Uncovering useful tidbits
- Understanding why information is power
- Strengthening your negotiating position

Your real estate agent and the sellers' real estate agent are great sources of information about properties and their sellers. Ask questions of them to find out the possible pitfalls of owning one of the homes you've tagged as a strong candidate. Another useful tool, of course, is the Internet, where you can frequently find useful information for free (or close to it) that can put you in a better position to negotiate a lower purchase price.

Would it be helpful to know that a home has been on the market for more than a year? You bet it would! Or that the basement floods every spring? It could certainly save you some money up front.

Invest a little time trying to get the whole history of a home and its owners to ensure you pay as little as possible to get your dream home.

Owners

Most real estate agents can give you some basic background about the sellers; the rest you can try to get them to find out from the selling agent or you can discern from your tour of the home. Some potentially useful pieces of information include the following:

What is the owner's background?	
Name	_____
Age	_____
How long they've lived there	_____
Whether they have children	_____
Where they work	_____
What they do	_____

At first glance, you might think these pieces of information are relatively useless when negotiating a better deal on your first home. The key is using this information to paint a complete picture of the sellers, including their lifestyle and why they're moving, so you can make them an offer they can't refuse—and is a good deal for you.

If you have the seller's name, try using Google. com to learn a little more about him or her. Has she been recently promoted to a major job out of town? Has she been named in an expensive lawsuit going to court soon? Is she suing the fire department for failing to provide adequate assistance in last year's fire at the house? You just never know what interesting facts will come up when you run a simple Google search!

Reason for Sale

Learning why a home is on the market will probably yield the most useful information of all. You may discover the sellers are time-crunched due to a job transfer or pending foreclosure, or that, with two young children, the sellers simply need more space. Of course, if you, too, have two young children, you may want to reconsider how long the home will be large enough for you.

Try to determine whether any of the following situations apply:

Why is the seller moving?
☐ To move to a larger home
☐ To move to a different school district
☐ To be closer to out-of-town family
☐ To transfer to another job
☐ Because he has already been transferred

continues

Why is the seller moving? (continued)

☐ Because he has lost his job

☐ To get married

☐ Because he is getting divorced

☐ Because they are having another child

☐ Because his employer is downsizing

☐ Because he is retiring

☐ Because his home was damaged by flood

☐ Because his home was damaged by fire

☐ Because the home is being foreclosed on

☐ Because the home is part of an estate

☐ Because the home is bank-owned

☐ Because the neighborhood no longer safe

☐ Because taxes are now unaffordable

☐ Other _____

Check your state's laws regarding what sellers are required by law to disclose to you about their home. For example, they may have to tell you that the fireplace doesn't work, but not that there was a murder in the house three years ago. It all depends on the state, so it would benefit you to ask some very pointed questions about the home's history and condition.

How Long on the Market

The number of days or months a home has been on the market may give you a sense of how willing the sellers may be to accept less than their asking price. Find out the following:

How long has the home been on the market, and why?
How many days has the property been in the Multiple Listing Service (MLS) system? _____
Was it was previously listed? _____
Have there been any price reductions? _____
Have there been any offers? _____
At what price? _____

One indicator of how long a property has been up for sale is in the photos. If the home has been photographed with snow on the roof and you're in the middle of summer, you know it's been available for at least six months, no matter what the MLS listing reports.

How Long Owned

Although not essential to the home research process, it can be interesting to learn how long ago a home was sold and for what.

There are some great online tools that provide basic information for free and more in-depth data for a fee—generally around $15.00. Check out these websites to see what you can learn, even if you don't pay for a report:

Where can you go for online sleuthing?

www.domania.com _____

Provides dates and sale prices when you type in an address. Free.

www.homeinfomax.com _____

Offers a complete report on owners, features, condition, and assessed value. Approximately $15.

www.intelius.com _____

Tells you all about a property, its taxes, its assessed value, and its owners. Approximately $15.

www.zillow.com _____

Shows aerial photos, the assessed value, and the values of homes around it. Free.

The only value of knowing when sellers have moved in is to gauge how much upkeep and maintenance they've done during that time. If no major projects were reported and a seller has lived in a home for 10 years, it would be safe to assume that some maintenance has been deferred—meaning you'll have to take care of it soon.

Assessed Value

You can easily find a home's assessed value on most MLS listings, but if you want to verify it, you can check with the county clerk's office. While there, you could ask to see the property's drawings, to confirm the home's size and scope.

What's it worth?	
Assessed value	_____
Date assessed	_____
Annual appreciation percentage	_____
× # of years since last assessment	_____
= Estimated current assessed value	_____

Keep in mind that some cities and towns assess properties based on a percentage of the market value. So if a home is assessed at $150,000, don't assume that $150,000 is the estimated market value. It may not be. If assessments are done at 80 percent of market value, then a $150,000 home is worth in the neighborhood of $187,500.

Price Paid

A number of sources can give you the most recent price paid for a home:

- The MLS system
- The county clerk's office

- www.domania.com
- www.homeinfomax.com
- Past issues of the local newspaper
- The seller's real estate agent

> Keep in mind that what the seller paid for the house—whether it was last year or umpteen years ago—isn't relevant to its current market value. What it might suggest, however, is a minimum price the seller would be willing to accept to sell it. (In a down market, however, that price may turn out to be on the high end.)

Finding Skeletons in the Closet

Although you are certainly eager to know about any major past problems with the home, so you can require that the seller fix them before you move in, sometimes they can be difficult to uncover.

A home inspector will find most issues for you, but if the seller has taken pains to cover up a problem, you may be out of luck. Here are some places to get the dirt on a home, so to speak:

Where to get information about a home

☐ The local police department: Ask about any police calls to the house, break-ins, or anything you should know about.

☐ The local fire station: Ask whether they have any records of being called to the property.

☐ Google.com: An Internet search may turn up similar police or fire calls.

☐ Sex offender list: Since registered sex offenders have to report their address, find out whether you have one living next door at www.familywatchdog.us.

☐ The neighbors: Ask the neighbors casually about any problems at the house that they're aware of.

Pending Projects

In some cases, there may be little wrong with a home's structure, but big changes may be brewing. If a development is being expanded, bringing more traffic to the street, that could be detrimental to the home's value. Or if a halfway house will soon be operating down the street, you may face a similar decline in value.

Ask your real estate agent about any of the following:

What negative growth projects are pending?		
	Yes	No
Nearby road widening	☐	☐
Development expansion	☐	☐
New building/development	☐	☐
Rezoning area to commercial	☐	☐
Expanded commercial area	☐	☐
Halfway house	☐	☐
New jail	☐	☐
Businesses shutting down	☐	☐
Public transportation rerouted	☐	☐
Other _____	☐	☐

Questions to Ask Your Mortgage Broker/Real Estate Agent

Was this property previously listed by another agent?

_____

_____

How long ago was that?

_____

_____

What do the disclosure laws require in our state?

_____

_____

What do sellers not have to tell us?

_____

_____

Are you aware of anything in this house that the seller has not told us about?

_____

_____

Have you heard of any new developments going in nearby?

_____

_____

Are there any commercial projects in the works that I should be aware of?

_____

_____

Notes/Observations

_____

_____

_____

_____

_____

_____

_____

_____

_____

_____

_____

_____

_____

_____

_____

_____

_____

_____

_____

_____

_____

_____

Chapter 8

The Finalists

In this Chapter

- Investigating condition concerns
- Estimating exterior repair costs
- Searching for interior weak spots
- Determining major and minor issues

Once you've zeroed in on a handful of desirable properties, it's time to start calculating the cost to repair any existing damage or address deferred maintenance concerns. If the seller hasn't been regularly maintaining the property, the cost to get it done in one fell swoop could be minor or it could be exorbitant.

Before you offer to pay a certain price for a home, make sure it won't cost thousands more to make it livable. Although you'll certainly get detailed information about a home's condition during a home inspection, you don't want to wait until after you've made an offer to start checking out major condition issues. And if you're comparing several properties, you'll want to tackle this step on your own to help decide which home will best meet your needs and budget.

The Exterior

By walking around the outside of a property, you should have a fairly clear view of certain elements to judge whether repairs may be needed. Be sure to focus your attention on the following exterior spaces:

What is the condition of the roof?

	Yes	No
Is it missing shingles?	☐	☐
Is it dipping toward the center?	☐	☐
Is it moss-covered?	☐	☐
Are there any visible holes?	☐	☐
Is the flashing tight around any chimneys or vents?	☐	☐
Is it over 10 years old?	☐	☐
Other _____	☐	☐

What is the condition of the exterior finish?

	Yes	No
Is the paint peeling or flaking on outside walls?	☐	☐
Is there rust around nails or bolts?	☐	☐
Are there stains in any stucco?	☐	☐

	Yes	No
Are there any soft spots in the stucco exterior?	☐	☐
Are there significant cracks in the stucco?	☐	☐
Is the wood consistently hard?	☐	☐
Do any pieces of wood break off when poked?	☐	☐
Are there significant cracks in the mortar between bricks?	☐	☐
Do the bricks need to be repointed?	☐	☐
Other _____	☐	☐

When dealing with wood siding, don't rely solely on your eyesight to determine whether there's a problem, because you won't see it. Take the time to press different pieces of siding to confirm they are not rotted or termite-infested, which would be suggested if the wood crumbles or falls apart when touched. Rotten wood is a big problem!

What is the condition of the chimney?

	Yes	No
Is the chimney standing straight?	☐	☐
Are there any missing bricks?	☐	☐
Is it crumbling in spots?	☐	☐
Are there cracks in the masonry?	☐	☐
Does it have a chimney cap on top?	☐	☐
Other _____	☐	☐

> Although you may not be able to get up on the roof and inspect the chimney up close, you can use binoculars to get a much closer look at its condition even from the ground. (Later you can hire a certified chimney inspector to be sure.)

Experts agree that water is perhaps the most damaging force, wreaking havoc on homes in places you may not yet notice. Pay attention to how water flows off of and away from homes for a sense of how protected the home may be from water damage.

What is the condition of the house's drainage?

	Yes	No
Are there gutters along the rooflines?	☐	☐
Are they clean or full of leaves?	☐	☐
Do they connect with downspouts?	☐	☐
Are there any circular depressions on the ground where gutters overflow routinely?	☐	☐
Does the ground slope away from the house on all sides?	☐	☐
Is there a nearby storm drain?	☐	☐
Other _____	☐	☐

Although you might not think to spend much time looking at the windows beyond checking for broken panes, windows are actually a good indicator of the quality of construction and level of maintenance. If you find problems here, be concerned.

What is the condition of the windows?

	Yes	No
Do the windows slide open easily and quietly?	☐	☐
Can you close the windows without much effort?	☐	☐
Are any panes broken?	☐	☐
Are the window sills hard, without mushy spots?	☐	☐
Can you see any water stains on the sills?	☐	☐
Other _____	☐	☐

What is the condition of the driveway?

	Yes	No
Are there cracks in the driveway?	☐	☐
Is it newly sealed?	☐	☐
Is the surface flat?	☐	☐
Can you pull easily into traffic from it?	☐	☐
Is it concrete?	☐	☐
Is it heated?	☐	☐
Other _____	☐	☐

Keeping a log of the defects you notice outside and inside will help you estimate the cost to repair and correct those defects later.

Interiors

In most cases, exterior defects will be more costly to repair than interior defects, but even small problems can add up to a big bill. Look carefully at all the rooms in the home, especially the kitchen and baths, where even small repairs can break the bank.

What is the condition of the ceilings?	Yes	No
Is there a "popcorn" finish on the ceilings?	☐	☐
Do you see any sagging?	☐	☐
Are any water stains evident?	☐	☐
Are there any that may have been painted over?	☐	☐
Is the paint even or is there a patchwork appearance where different colors have been used?	☐	☐
Are there any cracks?	☐	☐
Other _____	☐	☐

It is possible to remove or lessen the appearance of a popcorn, or heavily textured, ceiling if it bothers you. The main tool is sandpaper and a fresh coat of paint.

What is the condition of the walls?

	Yes	No
Are the walls standing at a 90 degree angle?	☐	☐
Are there nail pops evident?	☐	☐
Is there wallpaper?	☐	☐
Will it need to be removed?	☐	☐
Is the paint uneven?	☐	☐
Are seams visible?	☐	☐
Is there any crumbling?	☐	☐
Are there any holes needing repair?	☐	☐
Other _____	☐	☐

One concern about wallpaper on walls, besides the sometimes odd prints, is that it may cover problems you won't be aware of until you remove it. In older homes, wallpaper can sometimes act to keep walls structurally intact. Removing that layer can then cause big repair bills. Try to get information about how long the wallpaper has been up and how many layers may have been applied through the years.

What is the condition of the flooring?

	Yes	No
Are the floors level?	☐	☐
Do some rooms have carpeting?	☐	☐
Is the carpeting stained?	☐	☐

continues

What is the condition of the flooring? (continued)

	Yes	No
Is the carpeting worn?	☐	☐
Is the carpeting a neutral color?	☐	☐
Do some rooms have hardwoods?	☐	☐
Do hardwood floors need resanding and sealing?	☐	☐
Do some rooms have linoleum?	☐	☐
Is the linoleum worn?	☐	☐
Is the linoleum outdated?	☐	☐
Do some rooms have tile?	☐	☐
Are any tiles cracked or broken?	☐	☐
Is the grout in good condition?	☐	☐
Are any floors cement or concrete?	☐	☐
Is the cement in good condition?	☐	☐
Other _____	☐	☐

To spiff up a home's appearance, many sellers throw down clean, neutral carpeting, which may look fresh and new but shouldn't be expected to last long. Few sellers make a major investment in carpeting if they're moving out, so be prepared to have new carpeting installed in a few years.

What is the condition of the kitchen?

	Yes	No
Are the kitchen cabinets in good shape?	☐	☐
Is there sufficient storage space?	☐	☐

	Yes	No
Is there a pantry?	☐	☐
Is the countertop in good condition?	☐	☐
Are the appliances updated?	☐	☐
Is the "working triangle" of appliances laid out well?	☐	☐
Is the sink stained or scratched?	☐	☐
Is there space for a small table and chairs?	☐	☐
Can you pull up stools to the counter?	☐	☐
Is there sufficient counter space to work?	☐	☐
Other _____	☐	☐

Every kitchen has three essential appliances—a sink, refrigerator, and stove—that together form a "working triangle" that people move within when cooking a meal. The more steps you have to take between each triangle point, the worse the triangle design.

Although a total kitchen makeover can cost tens of thousands of dollars, it is possible to replace a laminate kitchen counter for a few hundred dollars, paint older cabinets for under $100, replace hanging lamps and lighting for a few hundred, and even put down a new linoleum flooring for not much more. You can really redo a kitchen on a budget—you don't have to spend big bucks to make a dramatic difference

What is the condition of the bathrooms?

	Yes	No
Is there any sign of water damage or leaks?	☐	☐
Is there a shower?	☐	☐
Is it large enough for an adult?	☐	☐
Is there a bathtub?	☐	☐
Is it in good condition?	☐	☐
Is the toilet a high-efficiency unit?	☐	☐
Is there ample counter space?	☐	☐
Is there storage space?	☐	☐
Is there a linen closet nearby?	☐	☐
Is the lighting sufficient?	☐	☐
Other _____	☐	☐

Infrastructure

The structure of a home probably indicate whether you're likely to find big problems inside, but not always. However, almost anything defective in the foundation or plumbing system is going to require a major cash infusion. Find out what you can about such defects before you make an offer.

What is the condition of the foundation?

	Yes	No
Are there cracks in the basement floor?	☐	☐
Is there any sign of water inside the basement?	☐	☐

	Yes	No
Are the basement walls damp?	☐	☐
Do you see cracks in the outside foundation?	☐	☐
Are there any cracks in floor joists?	☐	☐
Are there any defects in I-beams or support columns?	☐	☐
Other _____	☐	☐

Don't get too nervous about missing anything here because, if you're serious about buying this particular home, you'll pay for a home inspection later anyway. But taking the time to evaluate a home's condition gives you a general idea of how well it has been cared for.

What is the condition of the heating, ventilation, and air conditioning (HVAC) system?

	Yes	No
Is the furnace less than 10 years old?	☐	☐
Is the air conditioning unit less than 10 years old?	☐	☐
Is the water heater less than 10 years old?	☐	☐
Is there a programmable thermostat?	☐	☐
Are there radiators?	☐	☐
Do they all work?	☐	☐
Is the water in the home clear?	☐	☐
Does the water have an odor?	☐	☐
Is the home's water from a well?	☐	☐

continues

What is the condition of the heating, ventilation, and air conditioning (HVAC) system? (continued)	Yes	No
Has the water been tested for lead?	☐	☐
Is there sufficient water pressure in the shower?	☐	☐
Does the plumbing groan or knock?	☐	☐
Is the home on a septic system?	☐	☐
Has it been maintained regularly?	☐	☐
Is the lawn soggy above the septic tank?	☐	☐
Other _____	☐	☐

> The older a home and its infrastructure, the less likely it will have high-efficiency particulate air (HEPA) filters or be energy efficient. You may decide to make that investment for yourself, but unless the furnace isn't functioning or the plumbing has a leak, don't expect the sellers to be willing to make those upgrades for you.

Environmental Issues

Sometimes you may discover unexpected problems in a home that require correction before you move in.

Air there air quality problems?	Yes	No
Does the furnace have a HEPA filter on it?	☐	☐
Has the home been tested for radon?	☐	☐

	Yes	No
Was it within acceptable levels?	☐	☐
Are there any rooms with asbestos insulation?	☐	☐
Do pets currently live in the home?	☐	☐
Does a smoker live in the home?	☐	☐
Other _____	☐	☐

Are there other hazards?

	Yes	No
Has the home's paint been determined to be lead-free?	☐	☐
Have any damp walls been tested for mold?	☐	☐
Is there evidence of rodents?	☐	☐
Are termites in evidence?	☐	☐
Are bats or birds in the attic or crawlspace?	☐	☐
Other _____	☐	☐

Corrective Costs

Armed with your list of noticeable issues, it's time to figure out how extensive the repairs may be. Some problems can be easily corrected while others could become huge projects that interfere with your use of the home. Use this form to estimate how much work is required.

Major projects are those that cost more than $5,000 and minor ones can usually be done for less than that.

Are repairs needed?			
	None	Minor	Major
Roof	☐	☐	☐
Chimney	☐	☐	☐
Exterior finish	☐	☐	☐
Drainage	☐	☐	☐
Windows	☐	☐	☐
Driveway	☐	☐	☐
Ceilings	☐	☐	☐
Walls	☐	☐	☐
Flooring	☐	☐	☐
Kitchen	☐	☐	☐
Bathrooms	☐	☐	☐
Foundation	☐	☐	☐
HVAC system	☐	☐	☐
Air quality	☐	☐	☐
Environmental hazards	☐	☐	☐
Other _____	☐	☐	☐

One great resource for determining whether a remodeling project is worth the money is the annual *Remodeling Online* cost versus value report, which you can find at www.costvsvalue.com.

Questions to Ask Your Mortgage Broker/ Realtor

Do you agree with my assessment of the condition of this home?

_____

_____

Do you think the asking price is reasonable given these condition issues?

_____

_____

What do you think might cost more than I'm estimating?

_____

_____

What do you think might cost less?

_____

_____

How much time do you think these corrections will take to fix?

_____

_____

What percent of these investments, if any, do you think I'll earn back when I sell?

_____

_____

Which items should I expect the seller to make?

_____

_____

Notes/Observations

_____

_____

_____

_____

_____

_____

_____

_____

_____

_____

_____

_____

_____

_____

_____

_____

_____

_____

_____

Countdown to Closing

In This Chapter

- Reviewing the purchase agreement
- Conducting a home inspection
- Pulling together paperwork
- Looking for problems during the walk-through

Now that you've found an abode you love, you're nearly home. The next step is to present a formal offer to purchase the home, negotiate a fair price, schedule a home inspection, pull your paperwork together for the closing, and get ready to move.

But first things first—you need to let the sellers know that you're seriously interested in buying their home. That involves a purchase agreement outlining the transaction—how much you'll pay, when you'll take possession, whether any furniture or appliances are staying, and anything else that needs to be addressed.

Purchase-Offer Checklist

Before you sign on the dotted line of a purchase offer, read through the agreement and any accompanying paperwork carefully, to protect yourself from making a commitment you didn't intend to make. This is important because if the seller accepts your offer, it becomes a legally binding contract.

Items that should be addressed in your offer include the following:

What should your purchase offer include?

☐ The price you are offering to pay for the property

☐ A complete description of the property, including structures and street address

☐ Time allotted for response from seller

☐ Whether the sale is contingent on a mortgage commitment

☐ Whether the sale is contingent on the sale of another property

☐ Whether a deposit is being made and for how much

☐ Whether kitchen and/or laundry appliances are to stay

☐ Whether any furniture will stay

☐ Whether any window treatments will stay

☐ Contingency for a home or engineer's inspection

☐ Contingency for an acceptable radon inspection

☐ Contingency for an acceptable chimney inspection

☐ Contingency for an acceptable pest infestation inspection

☐ Contingency for an acceptable water test for potability and/or volume of water

☐ Contingency for an acceptable private sewage-disposal system inspection

☐ Confirming the sellers' insurance will be in place until closing

☐ Confirming that all disclosures required by law have been made about the property

☐ Any concessions you are asking of the seller

☐ Proposed place and time that closing will take place

☐ Proposed date of possession—generally at closing

☐ Provisions for who will arbitrate any disputes that arise

> An additional contingency buyers are smart to add to their offer is the approval of their attorney. This gives you the opportunity to get your attorney's perspective on the deal, as well as a possible way out if you are having second thoughts.

After submitting an offer on a home, you will likely begin the negotiation process with the seller. To prepare yourself for this back-and-forth bargaining, make sure you have the following in place:

What do you need to consider before negotiating?

☐ Your maximum: A decision regarding the absolute maximum you are willing to pay for the home

☐ Your nice-to-haves: Ideas regarding items you are willing to give up, such as appliances, closing cost contributions, or quicker possession

continues

What do you need to consider before negotiating? (continued)

☐ Comparable data: Information on comparables that back up the price you are willing to pay

☐ Preapproval: A preapproved mortgage

☐ Rationale for price deduction: Justifications for the lower-than-asking-price offer, which you have communicated to your agent

---

Although many buyers attempt to secure a great deal on a home by first throwing out a low-ball offer far below what comparables indicate is a fair price, it rarely works to their advantage. Not only does it insult the sellers, but it may make them less likely to want to negotiate at all, and you may lose out—especially if they receive a competing offer.

You can approach the negotiations in a number of ways. The strength of your local real estate market and the length of time the home has been for sale will help determine which strategy may work best:

Which negotiation tactics should you employ?

Strategy	When Effective
Make your best offer first	Works best in a hot market where you may not get the chance to make a second, follow-up offer
Offer near asking price	Works best in a strong market

Strategy	When Effective
Offer well below asking price	Works best in a slow market
Use timing as a bargaining chip	Works best when the seller is motivated to close quickly
Give up something	Works when you can trade something you don't really want for something you do
Resolve easiest issues first	Helps build consensus that can lead to a sale
Split the difference	Can work when the buyer and seller are close on terms and have gone through several rounds of negotiating

The Home Inspection

Your offer to purchase a home should be contingent on the results of a professional home inspection. It's important to know whether problems are lurking before you finalize the deal, so you can negotiate with the seller to have them corrected prior to your moving in. Otherwise, you're on the hook for it—and, depending on the problem, it can be costly.

Although home inspections are typically in-depth and require at least an hour or two to complete, the basic areas of the home that the inspector evaluates and rates include the following:

Which areas are covered in a home inspection?

Garage

- ☐ Roofing
- ☐ Siding
- ☐ Floor
- ☐ Vehicle door(s)
- ☐ Walls
- ☐ Door openers
- ☐ Ceiling
- ☐ Doors into house

Attic

- ☐ Roof framing
- ☐ Ventilation provisions
- ☐ Roof deck
- ☐ Insulation

Foundation

- ☐ Walls
- ☐ Concrete slab
- ☐ Columns
- ☐ Stairs
- ☐ Floor framing
- ☐ Railings
- ☐ Main beams
- ☐ Sump pump
- ☐ Any areas with signs of water damage

Electrical system

- ☐ Entrance line
- ☐ Distribution panel
- ☐ Main disconnects
- ☐ Electric devices
- ☐ Service grounding provisions
- ☐ Wiring
- ☐ Ground fault circuit interruptor (GFCI) test

Air conditioning

- ☐ Cooling system
- ☐ Condensation provisions
- ☐ Outdoor unit
- ☐ Ductwork
- ☐ Indoor blower/fan
- ☐ Thermostat

Heating

- ☐ Heating unit
- ☐ Burner
- ☐ Fuel line
- ☐ Combustion air provisions
- ☐ Vent connector
- ☐ Blower
- ☐ Distribution system
- ☐ Thermostat

Plumbing

- ☐ Water supply pipes
- ☐ Water flow
- ☐ Drain pipes
- ☐ Fixture drainage
- ☐ Exterior faucets
- ☐ Laundry sink
- ☐ Gas piping

Hot water

- ☐ Water heater
- ☐ Vent connector
- ☐ Gas/fuel lines
- ☐ Safety valve

Bathrooms

- ☐ Sinks
- ☐ Toilet
- ☐ Bathtub
- ☐ Tiling
- ☐ Flooring
- ☐ Walls/ceiling
- ☐ Lighting
- ☐ Vent
- ☐ Electric/GFCI

Kitchen

- ☐ Sink
- ☐ Floor
- ☐ Walls/ceiling
- ☐ Stove
- ☐ Oven
- ☐ Dishwasher
- ☐ Microwave
- ☐ Disposal
- ☐ Vent
- ☐ Cabinets
- ☐ Countertops
- ☐ Electric/GFCI

continues

Which areas are covered in a home inspection? (continued)

Home interior

- ☐ Ceilings
- ☐ Walls
- ☐ Floors
- ☐ Stairs
- ☐ Railings

- ☐ Windows
- ☐ Interior room doors
- ☐ Patio/deck doors
- ☐ Smoke detectors
- ☐ Fireplace

Home exterior

- ☐ Roof
- ☐ Siding/brick
- ☐ Landscaping
- ☐ Walkway
- ☐ Driveway

- ☐ Fencing
- ☐ Patio
- ☐ Deck
- ☐ Exterior doors

> Even if the seller doesn't offer it as part of the home sale, investigate whether a home warranty makes sense. The older the home is that you are buying, the greater the likelihood that a warranty would more than pay for itself during your first year of occupancy, especially if a kitchen appliance, garage door opener, or furnace fails soon after you take possession. Ask your real estate agent what the cost would be for your new home—it's usually only a few hundred dollars.

Mortgage Documentation

Although being preapproved for your mortgage requires little in the way of paperwork—a W-2 or pay stub, a list of debts, and a credit report—you'll still need to provide backup when you apply for formal mortgage approval. Be prepared to show some or all of the following when asked by your mortgage lender.

What documents should you be prepared to show to your lender?

☐ Copies of personal tax returns for the past two years

☐ Copies of business tax returns for the past two years if one or both borrowers are self-employed

☐ W-2 statements for the past two years

☐ Pay stubs for the last two to four pay periods

☐ List of all residence addresses for the past seven years

☐ Copies of the three most recent bank statements for all checking and savings accounts

☐ Copies of the three most recent statements for any brokerage, independent retirement account (IRA), simplified employee pension (SEP), or other retirement accounts

☐ A list of all credit cards and consumer debt with the balance and monthly payment required

☐ Documentation of alimony if it is being considered as a source of income

☐ Documentation of social security income if it is being considered as a source of income

☐ If a gift has been given to assist in financing the home purchase, a copy (or copies) of the canceled checks and a gift letter affidavit from the giver confirming the funds were a gift and not a loan

☐ Copies of any divorce decrees

continues

What documents should you be prepared to show to your lender? (continued)

☐ A complete copy of any bankruptcy proceedings and an explanation of the circumstances

☐ Copies of any lawsuits to which you are currently a party, whether as plaintiff or defendant

---

While you're in the process of finalizing your mortgage, steer clear of making any major purchases. Any additional debt could make it more difficult for your mortgage to be processed. Wait until after closing to go shopping for furniture or that new flat-screen TV.

Final Walk-Through

One of the last tasks to complete a few days before closing is a final walk-through of the property. This is your chance to do the following:

What should you look for during your final walk-through?

☐ Verify that everything you expect to stay with the house is still there—window treatments, appliances, light fixtures, furniture, rugs, and so on.

☐ Confirm that items that come with the house have not been replaced with cheaper versions.

☐ Make sure that the sellers' belongings have been removed—check the attic, basement, closets, garage, and so on.

- ☐ Inspect flooring that was previously covered by rugs or carpeting for flaws or stains.
- ☐ Confirm that repairs and maintenance promised in the contract have been done.
- ☐ Check that all appliances, light switches, and plumbing fixtures are in working order.

> If you will be stuck without housing between the time you move out of your current residence and close on your new one, ask the sellers if you can take possession before closing for an additional fee. Or ask your landlord if you can rent on a month-to-month basis until closing.

The Closing

You're in the home stretch when you get to the closing, where all your hard work finally pays off—in paper. Spending a couple of hours signing your name over and over and over may seem like a bit of a letdown, but once you're done and the sellers hand over the keys, you won't believe how exciting life gets.

During the closing process, which can take an hour or more, you'll be signing a stack of papers. These will include the following:

What do you sign during closing?

☐ The settlement statement, which is available before closing and lists what funds you need to bring to the actual closing

☐ Down payment details

☐ Closing costs

☐ Sale contract

☐ Mortgage papers

☐ Title or deed to the property

☐ Homeowners insurance policy

☐ Condo or coop paperwork

> Closing costs and down payments need to be made with certified funds, not just checks from your personal account. This requires a trip to the bank, which is why you'll want to request your settlement statement as soon as it's available, to ensure the checks you have written are in the proper amount.

Although the focus at the closing is on signing the reams of loan documents and contracts, you'll want to ask the sellers for some extra items (or find out where they were left in the home).

What other items might be handed off?

☐ Keys

☐ A blueprint of the home

☐ Any historical information about the property

☐ Warranty information on appliances and any recent repairs or replacements

Planning for the Move

As you near your closing date, you'll want to be sure to wrap up loose ends at your current residence as well as prepare for moving in to your new one.

To avoid being charged for rent and services you didn't use, make sure you inform current providers of your move-out date well in advance.

What is your timetable for moving?

Two to three months in advance

☐ Notify your current landlord in writing of your move-out date.

☐ Begin efforts to sublease your apartment if your lease term will not officially be up.

☐ Hire an attorney to represent you at closing, if you don't already have one.

☐ Schedule a home inspection.

☐ Schedule the closing.

☐ Formally apply for a mortgage.

continues

What is your timetable for moving? (continued)

Four to six weeks in advance

☐ Make arrangements with a moving company if you'll be using one.

☐ Complete paperwork for any school transfers.

☐ Arrange for home insurance to be in place on your new home as of your closing date, to cover you in case of an incident while you're moving in.

☐ Confirm with your lender that the mortgage process is on target for your closing date.

☐ Confirm with your attorney that all the paperwork is being completed in preparation for your closing.

☐ Start packing.

☐ Send out address change requests to magazines and other subscriptions and services.

Two to three weeks in advance

☐ Schedule a final reading with your utility companies—electricity, gas, water, cable, phone—as well as their transfer or turn-off.

☐ Request that utilities be turned on in your new home as of the closing date.

☐ Arrange for home insurance to be in place on your new home as of your closing date, to cover you in case of an incident while you're moving in.

☐ Schedule carpet cleaning in your apartment to occur a few days before closing.

One week before

☐ Schedule the final walk-through of your apartment.

☐ Schedule a walk-through of your new home before closing.

☐ Confirm moving details with movers.

☐ Confirm closing date and time.

☐ Ask for closing cost details, including check amounts to be written.

Day of the move

☐ Put pets in crates or a kennel during move.

☐ Get cash to tip the movers ($20 each is typical).

☐ Have a bag packed with clothing essentials and a box of cooking and dinnerware so you don't have to go searching for such items on arrival.

Hiring a moving company to relocate your belongings across town may cost a pretty penny, so consider paying the movers to move only the largest, heaviest, most unwieldy items. Then you're responsible for everything else, but you'll save yourself hundreds—maybe even thousands—of dollars.

You've probably heard horror stories about moving companies and items arriving damaged, broken beyond repair, or not at all. Fortunately, there are plenty of responsible, reputable moving companies, too, and they'll get your furniture to your home on time, in one piece. Here are some tips for distinguishing between the good and the bad.

How should you choose a moving company?

☐ Ask for referrals—from your real estate agent, your neighbors, and people who have recently moved.

☐ Request quotes from three to five of the recommended firms.

☐ Ask each firm for a state or federal license number to prove that it is legit.

☐ To check the background of an interstate mover, go to www.protectyourmove.gov.

☐ Ask the Better Business Bureau about any complaints, which you can review online at www.bbb.org.

☐ Read up on the moving process with a primer from the American Moving and Storage Association, available online at www.promover.org.

☐ Schedule times for company estimators to visit and scope out the items to be moved.

☐ Review written estimates provided.

☐ Consider paying for "additional valuation" coverage if the pieces you're moving are worth more than 60 cents per pound moved, because that is all the moving company's insurance pays you if something is broken en route.

Before you pay a mover to transport your huge overstuffed chaise, measure the doors into your new home to make sure it will fit. If there is a stairwell it will need to traverse, check that, too. It would be a shame to move it and then discover there's no way to get it inside. (This happens more often than you'd think!)

Questions to Ask Your Mortgage Broker/ Realtor

What do you believe is a fair price to pay for this home?

_____

_____

What is the bottom-line price the sellers are looking to sell for, if their realtor has shared that with you?

_____

_____

What are some items you think we can use as bargaining chips?

_____

_____

Is there anything you've seen during the walk-through that you would be concerned about if you were the buyer?

_____

_____

Notes/Observations

_____

_____

_____

_____

_____

_____

_____

_____

_____

_____

_____

_____

_____

_____

_____

_____

_____

_____

Glossary

It's important to be familiar with all the new terms being thrown around by your agent, your mortgage broker, the home inspector, and even your friends.

Avoid potentially costly misunderstandings by confirming that your understanding of different real estate terms is correct. Many of these you will certainly know, but others may be helpful to read through.

adjustable rate mortgage (ARM) A mortgage for which the interest rate is periodically adjusted based on several indices rather than remaining the same throughout the entire mortgage term, as is the case with fixed-rate mortgages.

amenity A feature of a home or property that enhances its value, such as a fireplace or commercial-grade oven.

amortization The breakdown of a debt into specific, scheduled payments, including principal and interest.

appraisal   The process of evaluating a home to determine its current value. It is typically conducted by a certified home appraiser on behalf of a bank or mortgage company.

appreciation   The increase in value of a property due to market conditions or value added by the sellers.

as-is condition   A statement indicating that the sellers are unwilling to make necessary changes to the property and that buyers must be willing to tackle such repairs and problems on their own.

assessed value   The value the town assessor places on a home for tax purposes.

bridge loan   A short-term loan that lets a home seller buy a new home before receiving the proceeds from the sale of the current home.

broom clean   A rather thorough house cleaning—countertops washed, bathrooms cleaned, and all garbage and remnants removed and hauled away. The term usually applies to the condition of a home prior to the final walk-through.

built-ins   Bookcases and storage units that are permanently affixed to the home, often around a fireplace or other feature.

buyer's broker   An agent hired by buyers to help them find a home. Without such an agreement, agents are bound to represent the seller first and foremost. With a buyer's broker, buyers pay half the commission in exchange for the knowledge that the agent is working on their behalf, not the seller's.

buyer's market   A real estate market that is generally favorable to those shopping for a home.

capital improvement   A permanent addition to a home that adds value, such as a deck or finished basement.

closing costs   Various costs, fees, and other expenses connected to the final closing on a property.

closing   The point at which real estate formally changes ownership. A variety of documents are signed by the seller and buyer. Various related charges and fees are also settled.

collateral property   Property used to back a loan. If the loan cannot be repaid, the collateral is sold to satisfy the payments due.

commission   A percentage of the real estate transaction that is paid to professionals for their service, the largest of which is paid to the real estate agent.

commitment letter   A formal offer to lend funds according to specific terms spelled out in the document.

common areas   Portions of a building, land, or amenities used by all residents of a condominium association, who share in the cost to maintain them.

Swimming pools, workout facilities, and parking lots are typical examples of common areas.

comparables Short for *comparable properties,* also known as *comps.* These are homes that have recently been sold and are very much like yours in terms of size, location, and features. In effect, they set the pricing parameters for your home by having preceded yours in the marketplace.

condominium A form of housing ownership where the living unit is individually owned but common areas are jointly held by all residents of the property.

contingency A condition placed on the sale of a home.

cooperative A type of ownership where residents become shareholders in the property, earning the right to live in a specific apartment unit.

deed The legal document that conveys title to a property.

depreciation A decline in a property's value. It is the opposite of appreciation.

down payment A one-time payment the buyer makes toward the purchase of a home. It reduces the amount the buyer needs to finance with a mortgage.

duty to disclose   Sellers are required to disclose material facts about a home or the neighborhood which would not otherwise be evident to the buyer. It is the seller's duty to make sure the buyer is aware of this information.

easement   A right to use a part of land which is owned by another person or organization.

equity   The difference between the market value of your home and the claims that exist against it, such as the outstanding amount of a mortgage, a home equity loan or line of credit, and other charges.

escrow   An item of value, such as documents or title to a property, held by a third party until specific conditions have been met.

Fair Credit Reporting Act   A consumer-protection law enacted to restrict how consumer credit information is reported and corrected.

fair market value   The price a buyer will agree to pay for a home.

Fannie Mae   The Federal National Mortgage Association, or Fannie Mae for short, sets guidelines for home ownership that buyers must follow in order to qualify for lower interest rate mortgages from their lender.

for sale by owner (FSBO)   A home that is being sold by the owner and not through a real estate agent.

foreclosure The legal process by which a property owner loses his or her interest in the property due to inability or unwillingness to pay the mortgage as required.

Freddie Mac The Federal Home Loan and Mortgage Corporation, commonly known as Freddie Mac, has guidelines for lending similar to Fannie Mae that buyers must follow in order to qualify for a Freddie Mac-backed mortgage.

home inspection An official inspection conducted by a professional to assess the structural and mechanical condition of a property as a condition of sale.

home staging The process of preparing a home for sale, making it as appealing as possible by cleaning, rearranging, and decorating it for maximum impact.

home warranty A service contract purchased to protect the seller from a major household expense while the home is listed for sale and up to a year after closing. Generally, major systems such as heating and air conditioning units, plumbing, and electrical, as well as appliances, are covered against breakdown.

homeowners association A nonprofit organization that manages the common areas of a condominium community or neighborhood.

joint tenancy A form of ownership giving each party full ownership if the other party or parties die.

jumbo loan A mortgage larger than $227,150, which are Fannie Mae and Freddie Mac's loan limits.

lease An agreement between property owner and resident outlining the rate of payment and the conditions under which the resident may use the property for a specified period of time.

lien A claim against a property that must be paid before the property can be sold, such as a mortgage.

lock-in The time period during which a mortgagor agrees to lend funds at a certain rate.

mortgage A document in which a property is used as collateral for a debt, usually to buy that same property.

origination fee The number of points, which are each equal to 1 percent of the loan amount, that the borrower must pay.

owner financing A purchase that the seller finances without the use of a mortgage lender.

PITI The sum of principal, interest, taxes, and insurance, which approximates the monthly cost of owning the home.

point One percent of the mortgage amount.

prequalification A process involving various financial calculations to determine whether a particular buyer is in a financial position to afford a home. As the term suggests, the prequalification process happens relatively early in the sale process rather than later. However, it doesn't guarantee a loan—other factors such as employment and credit history figure into whether a lender will actually approve a loan.

principal   The amount borrowed. Once interest starts to accrue, the principal becomes the balance due on the loan.

private mortgage insurance (PMI)   A form of insurance a buyer has to obtain if he cannot manage at least a 20 percent down payment. It is usually tacked on to a monthly mortgage payment. The going rate is between $50 and $100 a month for a medium-priced home.

purchase and sale agreement   A document drawn up to cover every single term and condition that applies to the sale of a home. Depending on where you live, the document may go by a slightly different name.

radon   A radioactive gas that has been found in homes throughout the country. Naturally produced through the breakdown of uranium in the soil, it can seep into homes through cracks in the foundation and other areas. Breathing radon in sufficient quantity has been connected with lung cancer and other illnesses.

sale lease-back   A transaction in which the seller transfers ownership of a property but then leases the same property back from the buyer.

second mortgage   A mortgage that is subordinate to the first mortgage, meaning that it will be paid off after the first mortgage if a default occurs.

survey   A legal drawing that shows the precise boundaries of a property.

title insurance   Insurance that protects the lender or buyer from loss if issues regarding a property's ownership arise.

title   The legal ownership of a piece of property.

walk-through   An exercise in which the buyer and seller walk through a home and the surrounding property in as complete a fashion as possible prior to the closing. The idea is to make certain everything in the home is the same as what was agreed to.

Research Tools and Resources

Books

Epstein, Lita. *The Complete Idiot's Guide to Improving Your Credit Score*. Alpha, 2007.

Fisher, Roger, and William Ury. *Getting to Yes: Negotiating Agreements Without Giving In*. Penguin, 1991.

Glink, Ilyce. *100 Questions Every First-Time Home Buyer Should Ask: With Answers from Top Brokers from Around the Country*. Three Rivers Press, 2003.

O'Hara, Shelley and Nancy D. Lewis. *The Complete Idiot's Guide to Buying and Selling a Home, Fourth Edition*. Alpha, 2003.

Reed, David. *Mortgages 101: Quick Answers to over 250 Critical Questions About Your Home Loan*. AMACOM, 2008.

Websites

Cyberhomes.com (www.cyberhomes.com) offers articles on buying and owning a home, as well as the ability to search more than 100 million property records, in addition to 2 million homes for sale.

Homebuying.about.com (homebuying.about.com) is another helpful resource about the process of buying a home.

Homeinfomax.com (www.homeinfomax.com), for a $15 fee, provides a thorough property overview, from owner names and addresses, assessed value, a property description, when it last sold, and so on.

Homestore.com (www.homestore.com) offers a central location for a number of information sources and services, including relocation search engines, mortgage calculators, and other handy tools.

RELibrary.com (RELibrary.com), the real estate library, contains tools for both buyers and sellers as well as an exhaustive list of links to other real estate websites.

Yahoo! Real Estate (realestate.yahoo.com) is a great general real estate resource with mortgage and loan links, information about homeowners insurance, and other information. You can also search for foreclosed properties here, too.

Zillow.com (www.zillow.com) lets you check out the assessed values of more than two million homes in the United States, as well as examine mortgage rates at many national lenders. It shows aerial pictures of homes, too.